This is a series of books about jazz artists, all of whom
have made either a significant contribution or have had an
impact on the jazz scene. Unlike some jazz books that
concentrate upon the detail of the performers' lives or
music, this series is concerned with much more. Here can
be seen the social background into which the subject was
born and raised and the environment in which his or her
music was formed. The social, domestic, racial and
commercial pressures that shaped the person are examined
alongside an assessment of other musicians who may have
influenced the artist or been influenced by them. Of course,
the music is not overlooked and each book carries a
discographical essay in which the artist's recorded output
is summarized and analyzed. Well-illustrated, the Life &
Times series of books is an important and long overdue
addition to jazz literature.

Louis Armstrong

HIS LIFE & TIMES

MIKE PINFOLD

SPELLMOUNT LTD
Tunbridge Wells

UNIVERSE BOOKS
New York

FOR FLO

In production in the same Jazz-Life & Times Series:

Louis Armstrong by Mike Pinfold
Dizzy Gillespie by Barry McRae
Billie Holiday by John White
Bunk Johnson by Christopher Hillman
Louis Jordan by Howard Elson
Gene Krupa by Bruce Crowther
Bud Powell by Alan Groves
Fats Waller by Alyn Shipton

Modern Jazz Piano by Brian Waite
Goodnight Sweetheart by Ray Pallett
Don't Fuss, Mr Ambrose by Billy Amstell

First published in the UK in 1987 by
SPELLMOUNT LTD
12 Dene Way, Speldhurst,
Tunbridge Wells, Kent TN3 0NX

First published in the USA in 1987 by
UNIVERSE BOOKS
381 Park Avenue South,
New York, N.Y. 10016.

©Mike Pinfold 1987

British Library Cataloguing in Publication Data
Pinfold, Mike
The life & times of Louis Armstrong—
(Life & times).
1. Armstrong, Louis 2. Jazz Musicians—
United States—Biography
I. Title
785.42'092'4 ML419.A75

Library of Congress Cataloging in Publication Data
Pinfold, Mike
Louis Armstrong, his life and times.
Bibliography: p.
"Satchmography": p.
1: Armstrong, Louis, 1900-1971. 2.
Jazz musicians——United States——
Biography. I. Title.
ML419.A75P55 1987   785.42'092'4 (B)
87-5954
ISBN 0-87663-667-9 (USA)
ISBN 0-87663-527-3 (pbk.) (USA)

Series editor: Bruce Crowther
Picture Researcher: Max Jones
Designed by: Words & Images,
Speldhurst, Tunbridge Wells, Kent
Printed & bound in Great Britain by
Robert Hartnoll Ltd, Bodmin, Cornwall.

CONTENTS

ACKNOWLEDGEMENTS

I would like to thank Bruce Crowther, John White, Bob Charlesworth and William Jules for their help.

The illustrations in this book come from the Max Jones Collection, Ian Christie, Bergt H. Malmquist, Howard Lucraft. Photo Files, Hans Harzheim, Jack Hutton, Sinclair Traill Collection, John E. Kuhlman, Jazz Music Books, Bill Russell, Eric Jelly, Nancy Miller Elliott, Charlie Mihn, Beryl Bryden, and from stills used to publicize films made or distributed by the following companies: Contemporary Films, United Artists, Majestic, CBS. Pictures are reproduced by courtesy of *Jazz Journal International,* the National Film Archive, Roy Burchell and *Melody Maker.*

Although efforts have been made to trace the present copyright holders of photographs, the publishers apologize in advance for any unintentional omission or neglect and will be pleased to insert the appropriate acknowledgement to companies or individuals in any subsequent edition of this book.

Frontiespiece:
Pops, taking care of business, while Peanuts looks on.
Louis and Peanuts Hucko, clarinet.

INTRODUCTION

'America's secret weapon is a blue note in a minor key. Right now . . . its most effective ambassador is Louis "Satchmo" Armstrong.'
Felix Belair, New York Times, 1955.

Louis Armstrong was the greatest single influence in the history of jazz. When one man is responsible for so many classic performances it becomes an impossible task to single out one occasion for special mention, but in 1956 I was witness to a particular performance which in its own way was very special.

For Louis, the 1950s were the most hectic and certainly the most successful years he had ever known. He and his All Stars were playing to mass audiences all over the world. In 1955 he had barnstormed across Europe on a triumphal tour; his concerts were sellouts wherever he appeared; jazz enthusiasts in their thousands flocked to see him. When he played in West Berlin, Germans and Russians alike sneaked over from the Eastern Zone to hear the great Satchmo. It seemed that everyone wanted to see America's lovable ambassador of 'good time' music.

In May 1956, along with hundreds of other eager jazz pilgrims, I trekked along to London's Empress Hall to see for myself the greatest of jazz legends. The Musicians' Union had only just relaxed their ban on American musicians and Louis was making his first appearance in the United Kingdom for twenty-two years. A buzz of anticipation filled the vast auditorium as we all settled back and waited for the historic concert to begin, but our moment of contentment was not to be won so easily. A seemingly endless procession of variety acts appeared on the centrally positioned revolving stage. Enthusiasm was not dampened, however, and the crowd erupted in a glorious salute when eventually the squat figure of Louis was spotlighted. The All Stars struck up *When It's Sleepy Time*

Down South and we heard the most glorious sound in jazz.

As the thrilling, fat tone of Louis's horn soared high in the cavernous auditorium so, too, did the spirits of each and every listener and smiles spread over the faces of the audience. New boy Ed Hall forced hoarse clusters of ragged notes from his clarinet, and trombonist Trummy Young, in fine declamatory style, pushed and cajoled in forceful *obligati* to Louis's lead. That evening we heard beautifully phrased, mature, trumpet playing at its majestic best. Along with his magnificent horn playing there was Louis's warm and joyous vocalizing and of course that wonderful hokum that upset so many American critics during the 1950s, but which Humphrey Lyttelton summed up so aptly when he wrote, 'Louis treads the tightrope between skilful showmanship and loss of dignity with consummate artistry.' Truly it was a momentous evening of never-to-be-forgotten musical thrills and unabashed showmanship—and we loved every single moment of it.

When finally we left the Empress Hall that night it was impossible not to dwell upon the contrast between Louis's triumphal return to London and the abject poverty of his origins in another city far away. As Louis's fellow New Orleanian, clarinetist Albert Nicholas, remarked: 'It's amazing how he came up from the ghetto and turned out to be the world's greatest.'

Louis's first British tour for 22 years.

8

CHAPTER 1

WHERE THE BLUES WERE BORN IN NEW ORLEANS

'The most exciting and wicked city in the South . . .'
Leroy Ostransky

New Orleans fits snugly into a crescent of the mighty Mississippi River some miles north of the Gulf of Mexico. The city is bounded on three sides by the river and to the north by an expanse of water named Lake Ponchartrain.

Today, New Orleans looks like any other large American seaport with ocean-going freighters lining the river, acres of container yards, busy thoroughfares and tall office buildings.

Tourists flock to this warm southern city: they come to indulge in the frenzied gaiety of Mardi Gras or to enjoy the garish nightlife along Bourbon Street. They can be found crowding the sidewalks in the Vieux Carré, admiring the still-attractive French-Spanish architecture, or in any one of many restaurants, sampling the Creole cuisine for which New Orleans is famous.

All this is a far cry from the mosquito-ridden French colonial settlement that Jean Baptiste le Moyne, Sieur de Bienville, and his compatriots established among the swamps of Louisiana in 1718. *Nouvelle Orléans* was originally inhabited by a motley assortment of French adventurers and deportees. Gradually, a more desirable element was introduced, but corrupt political leadership ensured that the city's reputation for being the 'most exciting and wicked city in the South, or perhaps the world' remained unchallenged for two centuries.

In 1762 Louis XV gave Louisiana to his cousin, Charles III of Spain. Spanish influence was sharply felt but relatively shortlived and in 1800 the colony reverted to French control. France's aspirations for Louisiana dissolved when, in 1803, Napoleon Bonaparte sold the colony to Thomas Jefferson. Thus,

New Orleans became another outpost along the lengthening frontier of the United States.

Tradesman, aristocrat, desperado and scoundrel, all were drawn to New Orleans. From the Old World came Frenchmen, Germans, Spaniards, Italians and Irishmen; Arcadians came from Nova Scotia, and settlers from British America. The city also proved to be the final destination for a great many slaves from Africa and the West Indies.

The people who converged on the burgeoning city, whether deportee, settler, vagabond, prostitute or high-born lady, had one thing in common: they came in search of a better life. Only the Negro slaves came without hope in their hearts.

Yeah, Daddy, Yeah!
Trummy Young,
Louis and Ed Hall.

Music always played a very important role in the lifestyle of New Orleans. In 1743, Pierre Cavagnial de Rigaud de Vaudreuil, Marquis and Governor of Louisiana, introduced to the city something of the pageantry and trappings, also the corruption, of the French court at Versailles. In the words of writer W. J. Cash, *Nouvelle Orléans* became 'a pageant of dandies and coxcombs'.

Entertainment proliferated, from lowlife bars, prostitutes' cribs and bordellos to high-flung banquets and balls. By the early nineteenth century New Orleans was famous for a variety of opera companies and for the French Opera House. Most popular of all was the social music played for dances, picnics and parades. On these occasions music was provided by both white and coloured ensembles. Inevitably, string orchestras and marching bands were in great demand.

Whereas the music of the white communities derived directly from their European heritage, black traditions of New Orleans related only partially to the Negroes' African origins. As late as 1819 Afro-West Indian music could be heard each Sunday in the city's Congo Square. Slaves were allowed to congregate there once a week, but by 1835 the music and dancing had become considerably diluted. This shift in musical style was due to a great influx of American slaves from Georgia and the Carolinas who brought with them a hybrid musical form. Plantation songs, such as *Get Along Home You Yellow Gals* and *Hey Jim Along,* were now performed in the square and by the middle of the nineteenth century African chants and West Indian incantations were only a memory, having merged with a myriad of white musical influences.

'From the beginning a hot-blooded, self assertive class, militant and proud, theirs was a firm and persevering belief that they were in every respect the equals of their Caucasian fellow-citizens.'

M. A. Rousseve

Bienville's Code Noir, or Black Code, was implemented in New Orleans in 1724. The Black Code was designed to regulate the life of the Negroes, particularly the interaction between black and white, but the ambivalent attitude of the French Roman Catholic or Creole community permitted cross breeding to develop. As a result, half-castes or *Créoles de Couleur* became accepted members of the community. Many coloured Creoles became successful businessmen, physicians, dentists, lawyers, and slave owners in their own right. Their freedom and social standing were unprecedented and without parallel elsewhere in America.

The coloured Creoles were able to share with their French-Spanish forebears a cultural enlightenment that was totally beyond the reach of the Negroes. Along with a deep love of the arts and of fashion, many of the coloured Creoles developed into adept, well-trained musicians. Their unique position allowed them almost every social advantage. By the mid-nineteenth century many were wealthy landowners and could afford to educate their children in France. Further down the social ladder coloured Creole merchants, real estate brokers, barbers, tailors and carpenters were accepted as almost-respectable members of the community.

The American Civil War wreaked havoc upon the special relationship between white New Orleanians and coloured Creoles, and the Louisiana Legislative Code No.111 designated all people of African ancestry as Negro. The fall from grace of the Creoles was swift and humiliating. Ostracized by the white community, their businesses failing and their lifestyles shattered, the coloured Creoles increasingly had to consort with those they regarded as low-bred blacks. For many of them, the once pleasurable pastime of making music was suddenly a financial necessity as they vied with the blacks for professional engagements.

Divisions between blacks and Creoles were strong, for whereas the blacks saw themselves as Afro-American, the Creoles were essentially French both in speech and outlook. With the benefit of over 100 years of education and training against the black men's long years of servitude and slavery, the Creoles considered themselves superior.

At first, the musical training of the Creoles made it possible for them to gain the better-paid 'coloured' engagements while Negro musicians rarely performed outside the confines of their own community. As the nineteenth century drew to its close, this situation rapidly changed. Sharing the stage with blacks became a bitterly resented necessity. As guitarist Johnny St Cyr recalled: 'The mulattos were actually more prejudiced than the whites were at the time.' Confirming this view, bass player George 'Pops' Foster in his autobiography explained: 'The worst Jim Crow [ie racial discrimination] around New Orleans was what the coloured did to themselves . . . The lighter you were the better they thought you were . . .' Foster remembered a black church in New Orleans where seating was arranged by colour, 'the lightest ones down in front and darker as you went back'. As American influence increased in New Orleans so the French language declined and even harder attitudes towards the colour line became evident.

Socially, New Orleans was a divided city: west of Canal Street was Uptown, the American sector; east of Canal Street,

Downtown, was where the French-speaking community lived.

Downtown New Orleans was home to America's most infamous vice district: the 'tenderloin'. Known as 'The District', it was officially recognized in 1898 when, in a desperate attempt to curb the frightening increase in vice and crime, Alderman Sidney Story proposed that the city should acknowledge the existence of prostitution but restrict such activities to a specific area. In this way Story hoped to ease the concern of the law-abiding citizens and contain vice to manageable proportions. Storyville, as it later became known, was restricted to thirty-eight Downtown blocks that housed numerous large brothels. Lulu White, Countess Willie Piazza and Josie Arlington were among the best known 'madames', whose establishments were particularly noted for their decorative splendour. In common with other more orthodox business establishments, they also practised discrimination; blacks were not permitted and the prostitutes were either white or octoroon.

Although white prostitution was restricted to Downtown, black prostitutes flourished on the other side of Canal Street. Johnny St Cyr, describing white Storyville, explained that in addition to the cribs and the good-time mansions there were eight cabarets or dance halls that used music. 'The rest of the area was just an ordinary neighbourhood ... The rough stuff went on a few blocks Uptown, around Perdido and Liberty. This is where the fights occurred.'

Louis Armstrong's view of the prostitutes was decidely romantic. 'Standing in their doorways nightly in their fine and beautiful negligees—faintly calling to the boys as they passed their cribs ... There were different shifts for them ... Sometimes two prostitutes would share the rent in the same crib together ... One would work in the day and the other would beat out that night shift.'

The poorest section of the city lay west of Canal Street and north of Rampart Street. This was 'back o' town', well within the black prostitution limits. The area along the river bank was 'front o' town'.

However poor they were, the burden of the back o' town blacks was eased by the musical sounds that pervaded the city, among which were the cries of street vendors. The blackberry woman, the crawfish boy, the washerwoman and the bottle man, all had their special 'songs'. White New Orleans was neither cut off from, nor unsympathetic to, these essentially black musical sounds. As the white musician Wingy Manone explained: 'A kid in New Orleans in my day was exposed to music, righteous music, from the day he was born. He learned it just like he learned to walk and talk. You come from the Crescent City, man, you *had* to have music in you.' White cornetist Johnny Wiggs remembered the street cries as being 'the dirtiest blues sounds I ever heard'.

No trip to present-day New Orleans is complete without sight and sound of a jazz band. The strutting, marching bands attended by a cavorting 'second line', and the jaunty Dixieland unit are both still very much a part of the city's attractions. Although depleted in number, they act as a reminder to the tourist of those halcyon days around the turn of the century, when Buddy Bolden was king and when the Creole orchestra of John Robichaux creamed off all the best social engagements.

Marching bands that played for a multitude of fraternal societies and lodges could always be heard in the city. Even the poorest black could enjoy the street parade and, at weekends, the picnics in Lincoln Park and Johnson Park or along the shore of Lake Ponchartrain.

Transport to the lake presented no problem as there were two narrow-gauge steam trains. One ran along Bienville to Spanish Fort, the other went west via Elysian Fields to Milenburg, and it was an easy matter to run alongside and jump aboard the slow-moving carriages. On arrival at the lakeside there was food for all, with music, music and still more music.

'When you come right down to it, the man who started the big noise in jazz was Buddy Bolden . . . I guess he deserves credit for starting it all.'
Mutt Carey

By the turn of the century, music-making in New Orleans needed more than the ability to read a simple score. Head arrangements, a dirty tone, the blues, were beginning to take precedence. A flamboyant black cornet player named Buddy Bolden was generally considered to be the first of the 'fellows to start jazzing', and the one who 'invented the hot blues'. Creole clarinetist Alphonse Picou recalled how his introduction to black music came about. A musician who had heard Picou practising at his home asked if he would rehearse with his band. Picou agreed and asked for his music. 'You don't need no music,' was the reply. 'That's impossible. What I'm gonna play? Just sit there and hold my instrument?' asked the perplexed Picou. 'Don't worry, you'll know,' was the answer, and so Picou went along. 'They were playing some good jazz music that I didn't know nothing about.'

14

The unrefined nature of this new music was distasteful to many legitimate musicians. The older Creoles could not accept this way of playing and began to lose out on the better-paid engagements. Many found they could no longer scrape a living from music. Big Eye Louis deLisle Nelson was one Downtown musician who fell in with the Uptown style. He was perhaps the first one to play 'hot' clarinet. 'Uptown they were more sociable and more like entertainers ... they played more rougher, more head, more blues.' Obviously, Nelson felt at home with the Uptown musicians and their music. As to the origins of jazz, he was quite definite. 'Blues is what cause the fellows to start jazzing.'

The Olympia Brass Band, still marching in the 1970s, surrounded by the 'second line'.

Pianist Joseph Robichaux, speaking to Tony Standish, was essentially in agreement with Big Eye Louis: '... the musicians who was mostly *known* from Downtown were fellows that read music, good musicians, and the ones from Uptown could play a little music and everybody would follow and they would play like that. During those times they called it *ragtime* and they played a more wild, ragtime style than the fellows from Downtown. But that didn't last so long because the fellows from Downtown were soon playing' the blues like the musicians from Uptown who, then in turn, started learnin' to read, and it got so that *everyone* could read *and* play blue-sy.'

White cornetist Wingy Manone acknowledged that although he learned the basics from his music teacher 'those coloured boys across the levee were the guys who really taught me to play'.

Describing the difference between black style and the music of the Creoles, Big Eye Louis explained to researcher-writer Alan Lomax: 'Jazz is all head music. Some players . . . have an idea . . . it kinda sound a little good . . . and somebody takes to that idea and writes it down. That's how riffs come about. You must handle your tone . . . There are a whole lot of different sounds you can shove in—such as crying—everywhere you get the chance. But you gotta do that with a certain measurement and not opposed to the harmony. Don't play like you're at no funeral. You've got to play with the heart.'

The bitterness that the upsurge of this crude music engendered in the older Creole musicians was well illustrated in conversations Lomax conducted with some of the Downtown elders. Violinist Paul Dominguez vehemently described how at first the Downtown musicians thought nothing of the rough Uptown music but gradually had to adjust. 'If I wanted to make a living I had to be rowdy like the other group. I had to jazz it or rag it or any damn thing. That's how they made a fiddler out of a violinist—me, I'm talking about.' Dominguez was quite certain who was to blame for this humiliating state of affairs. 'Bolden cause all that . . . He cause these younger Creoles, men like Bechet and Keppard, to have a different style altogether from the older heads like Tio and Perez. I don't know how they do it. But goddam, they'll do it . . . Can't tell you what's there on paper, but just play the hell out of it . . .'

As Lomax pointed out, the frustration and anger felt by Dominguez, bitter though it may have been, was tempered by admiration for those of his own kind who were able to assimilate so effectively the new musical code.

Reluctant as he was to 'jazz it', Dominguez himself was a survivor. In 1921 he was still leading a four-piece band at Tom Anderson's cabaret on Rampart Street. Included in the group was a young Uptown cornet player, and even the resentful Dominguez could not help but admire the playing of the friendly youth. His name was Louis Armstrong and he was soon to become a hot cornet king in his own right.

16

New Orleans and the surrounding townships have a reputation for producing good cornet players that goes back even before Bolden. Claiborn Williams led the St Joseph Brass Band as well as his own dance band around 1880. There was also Theogene Bacquet, lead cornet with the Excelsior Brass Band. Both were well known around New Orleans and by repute were great cornet players but strictly legitimate musicians. Bolden was the first of the 'hot' cornet kings.

Many tales have been told of Bolden's prowess. Jelly Roll Morton considered him to be 'the most powerful trumpet player I've ever heard'. Bunk Johnson recalled how Bolden's 'band had the whole of New Orleans real crazy and running wild behind it'. Bunk continued: 'They called Bolden's Band a "routineer" bunch, a bunch of "fakers". But, amongst the Negroes, Buddy Bolden could close a Robichaux dance up by 10.30 at night. Old King Bolden play the music the Negro public liked.' It is impossible to know exactly how Bolden sounded, but from the evidence of those who heard him it is reasonably safe to assume that he did not play jazz as it is recognized today. His was an intermediate style, something more than ragtime, which Manuel Perez played extremely well.

Perez was the best of the legitimate cornet players, considered by Mutt Carey to be a 'fine trumpet man', a better musician than Joe Oliver or Freddie Keppard, but 'he never was a hot man and he never professed to be one'. According to research by Sam Charters, Perez was a fine parade cornetist with a sharp, clipped attack.

Bolden however could fake and he played the blues, but by 1907 he had played himself out. His physical and mental health shot to pieces from wild living, he was committed to the East Louisiana State Mental Hospital where he remained until his death in 1931.

Heir apparent to Bolden's crown was a young Creole named Freddie Keppard. Although a poor reader, Keppard played a strong lead. Mutt Carey said of him: 'He'd play sweet sometimes and then turn around and knock the socks off you with something.' Jelly Roll Morton told Alan Lomax: 'He'd hit the highest and the lowest notes on a trumpet that anybody outside of Gabriel ever did. He had the best ear, the best tone and the most marvellous execution I ever heard and there was no end to his ideas, he could play one chorus eight or ten different ways.' Johnny St Cyr described Keppard as 'the first of the get-off men on cornet, a real pace setter and pioneer'. In 1912, still in his prime, King Keppard left New Orleans to join Bill Johnson and the Original Creole Band to tour the vaudeville circuit between New York and Los Angeles. It was this unit that first introduced the New Orleans sound to the rest of America.

Back in New Orleans the stage was set for another cornet player to lay claim to the kingdom. There were plenty of contenders; indeed, the city was spoilt for choice. There was the subtle phrasing and clear tone of Bunk Johnson or the gutbucket blues of Mutt Carey. If Evan Thomas from Crowley, Louisiana, had stayed for long in New Orleans he may well have claimed the crown, but he preferred to work the smaller towns. Alternatively, Creoles may have favoured the bell-like tone and sharp attack of Peter Bocage or Manual Perez. Brass band musicians may have preferred Henry Allen Sr, or the multi-talented Manuel Manetta, and the white sector may even have considered Nick LaRocca to be an ideal cornet lead. Two contenders, however, stood out from the rest. One was perhaps the most popular musician in New Orleans never to find fame outside the city.

Papa Joe (seated)

From all accounts, Buddy Petit, although small in stature, was a giant among horn players. Many have spoken of his creative and tasteful playing. His failure to capture the fame that seems to have been his due rests to a great extent upon his own irresponsibility. Barney Bigard said of him: 'Buddy Petit was so popular that he would take 4 or 5 jobs a night and go off and drink up the deposits. He'd work the best job and give some other little bands the left overs.' Mutt Carey confirmed this: 'Petit was a boy who had ideas . . . but let the liquor get the better of him . . . He was no high note man . . . Buddy always had a way of getting out of a hole when he was improvising.'

The other contender was a man whose first professional job had been with the Olympia Brass Band: Joe Oliver. According to Bunk Johnson, Oliver was a slow starter, and Oliver himself told trombonist Preston Jackson that it took him ten years to develop a tone. But before Keppard left New Orleans in 1912, Oliver had already staked a claim for supremacy. Pianist Richard M. Jones remembered how Oliver had been afraid of Keppard and Perez and lacked self-confidence: 'Practically overnight he woke up and started playing.' Keppard was pulling in the crowds at Pete Lala's Cafe in the District and Oliver was playing at the Abadie Cabaret just a block away. Legend has it that Joe walked out onto the sidewalk and blew his horn until people poured out of the other night spots. Going back into the Abadie, Oliver said with some satisfaction: 'Now, that—won't bother me no more . . .'

18

Johnny Wiggs, talking to George W. Kay, recalled seeing Oliver in 1916 and was impressed. 'I remember vividly seeing Joe Oliver standing in front of his band with his film-covered cockeye staring to the left and his brown derby over his seeing eye ... No other band had any meaning to me except Joe Oliver, including the white bands ...' To Mutt Carey, Oliver was simply 'the greatest *freak* trumpet player I ever knew. He did most of his playing with cups, glasses, buckets and mutes. He was the best gutbucket man I ever heard.' Many people thought Carey was the first to use mutes and buckets, but Mutt gave full credit for this to Oliver. 'Joe could make his horn sound like a holy roller meeting.'

After Keppard left, Oliver was the horn to beat in the cutting contests. Bands would travel around the city streets on the backs of carts and trucks advertising a dance or picnic where they were to play. Much rivalry ensued and each band would try to outplay the other. Louis Armstrong described how, 'On Sundays, a dance hall owner would hire a wagon for his band. And the wagon would go around the streets. Bass fiddle player and the trombone man sat at the tailgate, so they won't bump the others. Rest of the boys—drums, guitar, trumpet and so forth—sit in the wagon.' Louis, then an up-and-coming young cornet player, was a confirmed devotee of 'Papa Joe' Oliver and listened to him at every opportunity. He was to tell of a time when he was hustling coal to the crib girls in Storyville and was thrilled to hear the sound of Oliver playing across the street at Pete Lala's. 'I was just a youngster who loved that horn ... I'd stand there listening to King Oliver lead out on one of those good ol' good ones like *Panama* or *High Society*. My, whatta punch that man had.'

Like other musicians in New Orleans, Oliver played with a number of different bands including the Onward Brass Band in which he worked alongside Manuel Perez. Louis recalled, 'You never heard a brass band swing in your whole life like those boys.'

By 1917 Oliver was playing in Kid Ory's band and was billed as 'King' Oliver. The crown was his. The following year, Oliver, like Keppard before him, left New Orleans, accepting an offer to work in Chicago. It was the last the city would see of the great King Oliver. Now without a cornet lead, Ory asked Papa Joe's protégé, 'Little Louie' Armstrong, to take the great man's place.

CHAPTER 2

DOWN IN HONKY TONK TOWN

'Jazz and I grew up side by side when we were poor . . . I sure had a ball growing up in New Orleans as a kid. We were poor and everything like that, but music was all around you. Music kept you rolling.'

Louis Armstrong

There was a time when all self-respecting jazz fans knew the essential details of Louis's early life: born on the fourth of July 1900 in New Orleans, christened Louis Daniel Armstrong, he lived his first years in his grandmother's house on Jane Alley.

Detailed research by a number of eminent jazz historians, not least James Lincoln Collier, has revealed these details to be almost certainly false. All that *is* certain is that Louis was born around the turn of the century and that his early years were lived in grinding poverty. A child of a broken home (his father Willie Armstrong left before Louis was born), he was in turn looked after by a grandmother, his mother and the family of his uncle Ike Miles. For most of the time Louis was left to fend for himself in the toughest, most crime-ridden section of the city. Louis explained: 'My mother went to a place at Liberty and Perdido Streets in a neighbourhood filled with cheap prostitutes who did not make as much money for their line as did the whores in Storyville. Whether my mother did any hustling or not I cannot say.' Little wonder he quickly became streetwise and ended up in the Coloured Waifs' Home.

Louis was a breadwinner for his family at a very early age. The family consisted of his mother, Mayann, Louis, his younger sister Mama Lucy, and a string of 'stepfathers'. Despite their abject poverty, Louis would always look back on those days with genuine pleasure and affection. 'My mother believed in old fashioned remedies . . . if you looked a bit ashy and scratched your legs . . . couldn't afford vaseline she'd put axle grease on

Jane Alley, New Orleans.

us. Wasn't gonna waste that food money on cold cream, she'd go and grab one of those wheels and stick her fingers in the nuts and rub it off on your ankles.' His unquestioning acceptance of his lot, to say nothing of the grim facts of his early life, is remarkable. He recalled only the good points, the community spirit, the friendliness and the delicious 'make do' meals served up by his beloved mother. These were made from leftovers, probably purloined, from the kitchens of the city's eating houses.

His mother left a deep impression on Louis. One often repeated story describes how, when he was a small boy, his mother instructed him to collect water from a nearby pool. Returning with an empty bucket he told his mother that an alligator was in the pool. Calming his fears she told him that the alligator was more frightened than he was. Louis replied, 'If he's more scared of me than I am of him, Mama, that water ain't fit to drink.'

Even as a child Louis's good nature, friendliness and sense of fun were in evidence. Everyone liked the wild young street urchin. Recalling their first meeting, Sidney Bechet said, 'I got to like Louis a whole lot, he was damn nice.'

Louis showed an interest in music from a very early age.

21

Bass player Ed 'Montudie' Garland remembered young Louis following the brass bands. 'He could hardly walk when he started chasing after us. I knew him as a baby ... Louis used to sing on the streets for nickels and dimes before he started with that horn—I'm talking about when he was nine or ten years old.' Louis did indeed sing on the streets with three other waifs. 'I sung tenor on things like *My Brazilian Beauty*.' This early experience helped develop his keen ear for harmony and the group was certainly good enough for cornetist Bunk Johnson to take young Sidney Bechet along specifically to hear them sing. Bechet remembered, 'They were real good ...'

Louis followed all the bands around the city and heard Bolden at Funky Butt Hall. He recalled, ' ... we'd look through the cracks in the wall of Funky Butt. It wasn't no classified place, and ... some of those chicks would get way down, shake everything, slapping themselves on the cheek of their behind ...' Certainly he heard all the other great cornet players, Keppard, Perez, Bunk, and his hero, Joe Oliver. Although many musicians have said that Louis played a little before he went in the Coloured Waifs' Home, Louis was himself adamant that this was not so. In his autobiography Sidney Bechet reminisced: 'Of course Louis was playing the cornet a bit before he went into that Jones school, but it was, you know, how kids play. The school helped, it really started him up.' Louis concurred: ' ... it sure was the greatest thing that ever happened to me. Me and music got married in the home.'

The building that housed the Coloured Waifs' Home was built around 1870. It was surrounded by malaria swamps and was originally the Girod Asylum but was in use only briefly before the Board of Health closed it down. In 1907 the city allowed the Coloured Branch of the Society for the Prevention of Cruelty to Children to use it, and Superintendent Joseph Jones set about reclaiming the gutted, broken-down buildings. By the time Louis was sent to the Home, around 1913, it was struggling along on a hand-to-mouth basis.

In his book *Satchmo: My Life In New Orleans*, Louis tells how he was arrested for shooting off a pistol on New Year's Eve and sent to the Home where, under the tuition of the Waifs' Home Brass Band instructor, Peter Davis, he gradually progressed from playing tambourine to lead cornet. The Waifs' Band often played in the city's parks for social functions and in street parades. Preston Jackson heard Louis and remembered him being 'terrific even then'.

In his perceptive biography of Armstrong, James Lincoln Collier indicates the significance of this early brass band

Family Portrait. Louis, his mother, Mayann, and sister Beatrice (Mama Lucy).

training. Louis was taught the aims and techniques of the brass band musicians and the rudiments of cornet playing. As Collier points out, the top musicians of the brass band world excel in dazzling techniques, full of bravura and exaggerated dynamics. The freak style of a Joe Oliver with the use of mutes, buckets, growls and horse whinnies has no part in such training. Purity of tone, power, rapid and clean execution (things for which Perez was noted) were paramount. Louis learned the need for these qualities at the Waifs' Home.

Louis's stay there probably saved him from the life of crime that was the lot of so many kids raised in those back-o'-town gutters. As Collier says, 'It gave him a sense of possibilities beyond the streets of black Storyville. He could see now that there was something other than the unsettled moiling life of the prostitutes, pimps, and gamblers of the old neighbourhood, with its disease, violence, and dirt. There was another way to be.' Louis was to make full use of the chance he was given. 'Anytime a cat would lay off they'd say "Run get little Louie." I went up real quick because I was crazy about the music and pretty fast on that horn.'

When Louis left the Waifs' Home after almost two years he stayed for a time with his father, Willie Armstrong, but he missed his mother and sister and soon returned to live with them. The teenage Louis was something of a hustler, picking up work wherever he could as newsboy, milk roundsman and coalman. He also admitted that 'the boys I ran with had prostitutes workin' for them. They did not get much money from their gals, but they got a great deal of notoriety . . . so I cut in on a chick.' Eventually he was to marry a young Creole whore named Daisy Parker. Briefly, they shared a hectic and stormy relationship before parting. Whenever and wherever he could, he would play his horn and earn a few dollars. He had bought his first cornet, 'All beat up, holes knocked in the bell', at a local pawnbroker's for ten dollars. Joe Robichaux remembered how Armstrong would have to 'stop up the leaks with soap'.

Louis began sitting in with some of the crude blues bands in the lowest of The District's honky tonks. Johnny St Cyr remembered Louis 'playing at Spano's Tonk at Franklin and Poydras with Boogers on piano. They were playing the blues and *Sister Kate*. Then, however, they called it *Who Threw the Bricks on Katy's Head*. Just a few little things they had worked up. Boogers could only play the black keys of the piano. This was in the toughest part of town and Spano's was one of the roughest places down there, so I didn't go down there too often, or stay too long. But Louis was always so clean and neat. He

Johnny St Cyr.

24

*Kid Ory, Little Louie
and Johnny Dodds.*

would get all cleaned up and dressed up to his job at Spano's.
My brother would go up to Louis, and throw his arms around
him and kiss him. This would embarrass Louis and he'd say,
"Don't do that, people will think I'm funny." '

Louis's musicianship rapidly improved and he developed into
a good blues player. Joe Robichaux remembered 'if Louis
wanted to play something fast he played the blues fast, and
when they wanted somethin' slow he'd play the blues slow. I
mean he was strictly a blues man then.' Mutt Carey
corroborates this and gives an indication of the quality of Louis's
blues playing. 'When I left New Orleans Louis was just a
beginner. He had just gotten out of the Waifs' Home and he
was a coming trumpet man then. I remember when Louis came
out to Lincoln Park . . . to listen to the Kid Ory Band. I was
playing trumpet with the Kid then and I let Louis sit in my
chair. Now at that time I was the *Blues King* of New Orleans
and when Louis played that day he played more blues than I
ever heard in my life. It never did strike my mind that blues
could be interpreted so many different ways. Every time he
played a chorus it was different and you know it was the
blues . . . yes it was all blues . . .'

It was around this time that Louis met up with Black Benny,
a noted drummer and even more noted villain. Benny spent
most of his life in prison, being let out only for street parades
and other musical functions. An infamous character, he took
a liking to the young musician and re-introduced Sidney Bechet
to Louis. Bechet remembered that Benny said to him one day,
' "You think you can play. But I know a little boy right around
the corner from my place, he can play *High Society* better than
you." So I said, "Well, I'd like to see that boy." . . . we went,

25

and it was Louis. And I'll be doggone if he didn't play *High Society* on the cornet . . . it was originally a piccolo part but it was done . . . by Picou on clarinet. It was very hard for clarinet to do, and really unthinkable for cornet to do at those times. But Louis, he did it.'

Johnny St Cyr took credit for introducing Louis to King Oliver, who was looking for a substitute cornet to take over at Pete Lala's Cabaret while he worked with the Magnolia Band. St Cyr recalled, 'Louis had a wonderful ear and he learned Oliver's repertoire from him in about three days.' Armstrong, recalling this job in his autobiography, tells how Lala wanted him to use a mute but he did not understand and played open horn. Consequently, at the end of the evening, Lala paid him off. St Cyr remembers the incident rather differently: ' . . . old man Lala had a limp and he would come across the floor, limping and shaking his finger at Louis . . . After he had turned his back, Louis would go into a little dance which would end up with him taking a few steps with a limp and shaking his finger just like the old man. This of course would bring the house down. Louis was always a comedian . . .'

Joe Oliver and Louis quickly became close friends. The older man, noted for his truculence, seems to have taken a shine to the eager youth and paid for a new cornet for Louis and loaned him money from time to time. Louis said of Oliver, 'He was the one who taught me after I left the Home, I listened to the others, but he gave me the tuition—I used to run errands and things for his wife. In my day he was the top man, Buddy Bolden was the great man when Joe was a kid. Joe was the most creative trumpet player I ever heard.' Louis always insisted that it was Oliver who influenced his early playing and not Bunk Johnson as Bechet and Johnson both claimed later. The truth is probably as Louis stated: he listened to and played with so many of the great New Orleans musicians that consciously or unconsciously he picked up a great deal from them all. Certainly he played with Perez, with Oscar Celestin, and with Mutt Carey, and it is well established (and confirmed by Louis) that he followed Bunk around. But none of them took an interest in him as did Papa Joe. As Russell Davies has observed, 'What Oliver *showed* Louis is of little of consequence compared with what he *heard* in Oliver's playing.'

When Oliver left New Orleans in 1918 Louis took his place in the Kid Ory band. By this time Louis was one of the best cornet players in the city, perhaps on a par with Buddy Petit. Cornet players Chris Kelly and Punch Miller were still in the Army and Louis's competition at the time came from Kid Rena,

Kid Shots Madison and Bunk.

Kid Shots Madison, Lee Collins, Maurice Durand, Sam Morgan and Herb Morand. Although all were fine players none could compete with Louis.

At this juncture, Louis's career took a course that temporarily removed him from New Orleans: he joined the Fate Marable band aboard the Mississippi riverboat SS *Sydney*. 'There was a saying in New Orleans,' drummer Zutty Singleton recalled. 'When some musician would get a job on the river-boats with Fate Marable, they'd say, "Well you're going to the conservatory." That's because Fate was such a fine musician and the men who worked with him had to be really good.'

For many years the Mississippi riverboats had been an integral part of the internal transport system of the United States, but with the coming of the railroad their importance began to falter. The boats of the Streckfus Lines were originally working vessels but by 1908 were being converted for use as excursion boats. The Lines were run by the Streckfus brothers Roy, Joseph, Jack and Verne, and one of their first innovations was to provide entertainment for the passengers and this included music for dancing.

Paddle steamers with such evocative names as *Dixie Belle*, *Ben Hur*, *Capitol*, and *Belle of the Bends* cruised the river from Davenport, Iowa, in the North to New Orleans in the South with ports of call at Cairo, Memphis, St Louis, Natchez, and Baton Rouge. The vessels have been described as 'floating palaces with lounges, restaurants and luxurious ballrooms', but evenings aboard the steamers often ended with little of the romanticism that these descriptions suggest. Many were shattered by vicious brawls and arguments. At such times the gentlemen of the orchestra were expected to play on regardless.

St Louis was the headquarters of the Streckfus Empire, and pianist Fate Marable from Paducah, Kentucky, was employed to play the calliope (a large steam organ) and to lead a dance band aboard one of the vessels. Danny Barker recalled, 'All over the river Fate Marable had a fabulous reputation.' Musician Jerome Don Pasquall told Thornton Hagert and Frank Driggs, 'Fate was a very good musician and well schooled.'

When he first played for the Streckfus brothers, Marable led an all-white band (he was himself very light-coloured) but in 1917 he employed, for the first time aboard the boats, an all-black unit. They came from his home town of Paducah, but as Marable explained, 'Although they played real nice they could not compare to the New Orleans boys.' It was not that the New Orleanians were technically superior, simply that they were excitingly different. Marable had been educated in New Orleans and was familiar with the music of the city. 'We were going in and out of New Orleans all the time and I began to notice the type of music they were playing then. It just got under my skin.'

In 1918 Marable booked a New Orleans band and it was sensational. In his biography, drummer Harry Dial, recalling this Marable band, said of them, 'The music they played was the most exciting thing I'd heard in my life at that time.' Baby Dodds, who played drums with the band, remembered being embarrassed because the people sat and stared at them. 'They saw Negro roustabouts but had never seen a Negro with a tie and collar on, and a white shirt, playing music. They just didn't know what to make of it. But they really liked it.' Jerome Don Pasquall described how the passengers were segregated. It 'was not a Jim Crow arrangement but most of the time they had a strictly white patronage.' Baby Dodds reminisced how in St Louis they would give special excursions for the Negroes every Monday. 'It was one of the most wonderful things you've ever seen ... we got such a kick out of it because it gave us a free kind of sensation for working. We worked all week for the white people and this one night we could work for coloured ... we were free to talk to people and the people could talk to us.'

Certain musicians have claimed that they arranged for Louis to join the band, but Marable himself recalled, 'When I heard Louis playing with Kid Ory at Co-operative Hall in New Orleans I knew right away I wanted him in my band.' Baby Dodds told Larry Gara, 'Louis was playing with the Ory band. So was my brother John. So I was fighting to get Louis on the boat, and my brother was fighting to make him stay with Ory.' Johnny St Cyr also remembered that Louis had 'gone into hock to Ory for a new cornet ... Ory said he couldn't take his horn because it wasn't paid for. Louis came around very sad, said he couldn't make it as he would have no instrument.' Streckfus was persuaded by the musicians that Louis was the man the band needed and paid for a new horn which Louis repaid weekly.

The change of surroundings had a great impact on Louis who was until then very much a home-bird. On arrival in St Louis, he gazed open-mouthed at the tall buildings and wondered if he dare ask what they were. Finally he plucked up the courage and asked Marable, 'What are all those tall buildings? Colleges?' 'Aw, boy,' Fate answered, 'don't be so damn dumb.' Ruefully, Louis later wrote, 'Then I realized I should have followed my first hunch and kept my mouth shut.'

A strict disciplinarian, Marable insisted that his musicians should read music. The band's repertoire consisted of all the

Fate Marable and his Riverboat Orchestra aboard the SS. Capitol. From the left: Henry Kimball, Boyd Atkins, Johnny St Cyr, David Jones, Norman Mason, Louis, George Brahear, Baby Dodds.

popular tunes of the day: *Jelly Roll Blues* and *Dardanella* intermingled with *Apple Blossom Time, Alice Blue Gown, Roses of Picardy* and *Ain't We Got Fun*. It was an excellent training ground and, as always, Louis made good use of his time. Aided by Joe Howard and especially Davy Jones, both well-schooled musicians, he soon became a competent reader. Louis recalled, 'Davy Jones, who played mellophone and sax . . . he helped me. When he got to know me he gave me lessons in reading music.'

Occasionally the musicians would have time off in St Louis and would sit in with the local bands. Baby Dodds was to recall, 'Everybody that was working the boat was known there and Louis and I used to travel together most of the time. And when we'd sit in there, we'd break it up. Naturally I knew how to work with Louis and Louis knew how to work with me, so it turned out very nice.'

Jerome Don Pasquall, at the time a resident musician of St Louis, remembered: 'When we first heard Louis, it was a revelation. To us we thought there was no jazz trumpet as good as Charlie Creath. Charlie used to swing the lead in such a way that he never got too far away from the melody, whereas Louis, with all that terrific technique of his (like clarinet almost), would play so many notes you'd be thrilled and forget all about the melody.' St Louis trumpet player Dewey Jackson, recalling Louis sitting in with the local musicians, said, 'Man! I never forget that trumpet. They played *High Society* and the trumpet takes four, five choruses and *hot*! I never know anybody play a trumpet like that. Later I find out it's Louis playing . . . I say to Creath. "Sorry Charlie, but *there's* the greatest trumpet player in the world." ' Marge Creath, Charlie's sister, remembered Louis at that time to be very quiet and shy. Jerome

Don Pasquall agreed: 'He was always a modest fellow, never boastful and always praising the other guy—the sort of person you'd figure would go back home, settle down and raise a big family. No one could have foreseen the dizzy heights which he has reached since then.'

Evidently Louis's sense of fun had not deserted him. Johnny St Cyr remembered that Fate Marable had a little Ford car which he kept aboard the paddle steamer so that he could get around each town when they docked. 'One evening several of us were going up Canal Street with him and we almost hit a woman who was walking across the street. Louis said, "You'd better watch out, you'll get arrested for emergency." We all said, "Emergency, what's emergency?" Louis said, "You hit that woman and you'll soon find out what emergency is." '

Baby Dodds remembered that even then Louis had a flair for thinking up oddball phrases that were later to become a part of the general jazz vocabulary. 'He used certain expressions on the riverboats like, "Come on you cats" and "Look out there, Pops" and the like. These were his own ideas. I had never heard such words as, "jive" and "cat" and "scat" used in New Orleans.'

Louis and Baby Dodds left the riverboats in 1921. Dodds said that Streckfus wanted them to play differently, 'They wanted us to beat a different time . . . Well we were the stars on the boat . . . why monkey with us?' Jerome Don Pasquall, who was by then a member of the band, remembered that during 'the summer of 1921 Captain Joe Streckfus started listening to the records of Paul Whiteman who had really become very popular . . . He would try to get us to emulate Whiteman's trumpet man Henry Busse and the rest of the band. But at that point, Louis and Baby Dodds seemed to lose interest . . .'

Louis returned to New Orleans where he played with Paul Dominguez at Tom Anderson's cabaret. Later he moved to the Fernandez Club to play with Zutty Singleton and also had regular engagements with Celestin's Tuxedo Band.

Storyville had been closed in 1917 at the request of the Secretary of the US Navy, but although many musicians had moved on, there were, in the summer of 1922, still many working bands in New Orleans. Louis might well have continued to live and play out his career there, as Jerome Don Pasquall suggested, but he received an all-important telegram from Joe Oliver asking him to join his band in Chicago. Many people tried dissuading Louis from going but as he was later to write there was little chance of that. 'Yeah man, I'm going up to Chicago to play with my idol, Papa Joe!'

CHAPTER 3

CHICAGO BREAKDOWN

'If you think this country ain't dry just watch 'em vote. If you think this country ain't wet just watch 'em drink. You see when they vote it's counted. When they drink it ain't.'

Will Rogers

The first important temperance pamphlet in America was produced in 1784, but by the time of the Civil War in 1861 only thirteen states had tried prohibition laws. This number was reduced after the war to three, and it was not until the foundation of the Women's Christian Temperance Union in 1873 and the Anti-Saloon League in 1887 that the movement took on a disciplined form. Social reformers of all persuasions joined forces to fight the evils of drink in the conflict 'Wet versus Dry'. The closure of vice areas was seen as an important step in the struggle towards complete prohibition of liquor.

In 1911 the Eversleigh Club in Chicago's Levee District was closed down. The Eversleigh sisters, Minnie and Ada, had opened their establishment in 1900, and by repute it was the most lavish brothel, not only in Chicago but in the whole of America. The celebrated New Orleans entertainer Tony Jackson regularly performed there.

In 1912 the entire Levee vice area was officially closed down when a grand jury disclosed the connections between local politicians and vice syndicates on Chicago's South Side. One of several officially tolerated vice areas in Chicago, the Levee district was controlled by two politicians. These were the unlikely-named Michael 'Hinky Dink' Kenna and 'Bathhouse' John Coughlan, both of whom owned saloons and dives in the district. They could often be located at Ike Bloom's notorious Freiberg's Dance Hall where politicians, businessmen and mobsters regularly exchanged confidences. Bloom was partner to Chicago's vice boss, Big Jim Colosimo. It was Colosimo who first introduced the infamous Johnny Torrio to Chicago's underworld. Torrio, a shrewd organizer, was to establish a basic underworld territory system which still operates in America.

In 1915 Mayor Carter Harrison appointed Major M.C.L. Funkhouser as head of a Morals Division within the Chicago Police Department. The Mayor also revoked Colosimo's and Bloom's licenses. Within eighteen months the chief of the Morals Squad was stabbed (after refusing a substantial bribe) and a squad sergeant killed. It took Bloom sixteen months and Colosimo five months to regain their licenses, but by then Chicago had elected Big Bill Thompson as Mayor.

Thompson fought the election on a reform ticket but, upon being elected, made it abundantly clear that Chicago would remain a wide-open city. Thompson's influence upon the illegal aspects of Chicago life led directly to the growth of crime and inadvertently to the wealth of jazz to be found in the city in the next decade.

Social reformers rejoiced when, in the battle of Wet versus Dry, the Drys gained an unexpected but resounding victory. In 1920 the 18th Amendment to the Constitution of the United States (the Volstead Act, commonly known as Prohibition) was passed and the prohibition of liquor became a reality. Billy Sunday, the hell and damnation evangelist, ceremoniously held a mock funeral for 'John Barleycorn'. Sunday's jubilation was premature; three months before the 18th Amendment became effective, liquor worth half-a-million dollars had already been stolen from government warehouses. Some states openly nullified the law and the governor of New Jersey promised to make the state 'wetter than the Atlantic Ocean'. Custom departments could barely interrupt the flow of smuggled booze. The public openly flouted the law and agents of the Prohibition Bureau became the most despised and resented officials in the country.

It was not until six months after the Volstead Act had become law that underworld schemer Johnny Torrio turned his full attention to the possibilities of the new liquor laws. Torrio had superseded Colosimo as vice boss in Chicago by simply eliminating the opposition. Colosimo was shot dead at his café on South Wabash Avenue. Torrio was business partner to brewery boss Joseph Stenson and this liaison furnished him with both a veneer of respectability and contacts in high places. He was able to take over the discontinued breweries and instigate a bootleg industry of gigantic proportions.

Although Torrio was the instigator it was his second in command, Al Capone, who reaped the benefits of prohibition when he succeeded Torrio to become overlord of organized crime in Chicago in the Roaring Twenties.

By 1922 the gradual migration of many thousands of Negroes from the Southern states to the Northern industrial cities, and in particular to the city of Chicago, increased to a flood. There were many reasons for the mass exodus, chief among them the general lack of employment and the intolerable Jim Crow attitudes of an embittered and belligerent white community. Additionally, there was the closure of vice and lowlife areas such as Storyville; many cotton crops were ravaged by the boll weevil; and there was feedback from earlier migrants telling of jobs and better pay. The black newspaper, the *Chicago Defender*, helped too: 'If you can freeze to death in the North and be free why freeze to death in the South and be a slave.'

Chicago was a general centre of industry with a floating community of itinerant workers searching for jobs in the stockyards and steel mills. The hub of the American railroad system, Chicago was also a water transport centre connecting inland systems with the international trade routes. People looking for work naturally gravitated to Chicago. Before 1917 it had been the immigrants from Europe—Irish, German, Scandinavian, Jewish and Italian—who settled there. These immigrants were at first willing to work for a pittance, but gradual resentment subjected Chicago to much industrial unrest and riots.

The combination of World War I and the resultant cutback in European immigration left a vacuum which, from necessity, had to be filled by blacks. Agents were sent south to entice black workers with free transport and suggestions that Chicago would bid them all welcome. However, the Negroes were merely tolerated from necessity, and in 1917 the first racial disturbances were recorded in Chicago.

Does Jazz put the sin in syncopation?
Anne Shaw Faulkener

Chicago was introduced to ragtime piano at the World's Fair of 1893. The earliest known New Orleans musicians to play in the Windy City were the legendary pianists Tony Jackson and Jelly Roll Morton—Jackson in 1908 and Morton in 1910. By 1911 the black clarinetist Wilbur Sweatman was leading a very popular band at the Grand Theatre. But it was not until the Original Creole Band, who were touring the Orpheum theatrical circuit, appeared at the Grand that Chicago first heard a New Orleans ensemble. The band was billed as 'an organization composed of past master musicians and screaming comedy'. The *Chicago Defender* critic, Tony Langston, wrote, 'The members of the band know how to extract the most weird effects from their various instruments and are assisted by a character comedian of good voice. The act was a novel one and went well.' The comedian was H. Morgan Prince and the band featured the cornet of Freddie Keppard and the clarinet playing of George Bacquet.

In 1915 a white New Orleans band, led by trombonist Tom Brown, played at the Colosimo-backed Lamb's Cafe. After Brown's band another white band led by drummer Johnny Stein arrived in Chicago. Booked by entrepreneur Harry James, the band included cornet player Nick LaRocca. After various personnel changes the band left Chicago for New York where they caused a sensation. Now named the Original Dixieland Jazz Band, they became the first New Orleans group to record and were instrumental in introducing jazz music to the rest of the world.

Among the black New Orleans musicians who had settled in Chicago by 1917 was the cornet player Sugar Johnny Smith. Smith led the New Orleans Creole Band at the Pekin Cafe and at Dreamland. Wellman Braud, who played bass with the band, remembered: 'Lil Hardin was with us then . . . People would shout in their chairs . . . We open the Pekin in 1917. Played at Dreamland until one o'clock and then played at the Pekin till six in the morning.' Speaking of her time with the New Orleans Creole Band, Lil Hardin recalled, 'Montudie [Ed Garland], Tubby [Hall] and I beat out a background rhythm that put the Bechuana tribes of Africa to shame.'

A considerable amount of support for the election of Big Bill Thompson came from the black community. Colosimo, Torrio and Capone were not the only underworld czars in Chicago. The earliest black vice boss was John 'Mushmouth' Johnson, who was known to have paid off politicians Kenna and Coughlan as insurance against his establishments being raided. After Johnson's premature death he was succeeded by a number of black underworld figures, among them Bob Motts, Henry Teenan Jones and Daniel M. Jackson. Motts owned the Pekin Theatre and Jones opened the Elite Theatres Nos. 1 and 2, two blocks apart on State Street. The Pekin and the Elite Theatres together with the Grand, Monogram and Vendome Theatres, the Royal Garden (later called Lincoln Garden) and Bill Bottoms' Dreamland, the DeLuxe, Fiume and Sunset Cafes, formed the nucleus of the nightlife that lit up the South Side of Chicago in the 1920s. All these nightspots were mob-owned. Jazz was now inextricably linked with vice and crime.

The South Side in the 1920s was more than simply a jazz centre, it was a centre for all forms of black entertainment. Edward M. Reeves has written: 'The Black Belt of Chicago was not an imaginary line, drawn to encircle the city's growing coloured population: it was a ghetto, a fact of life; a nuisance; a haven; a rendezvous; heaven for some folks, the den-of-iniquity for others.' Theatrical and musical talent exerted considerable influence on the city. Along the four-block section of State Street, between 31st and 35th Streets (known as 'The Stroll'), black performers, actors and musicians could be found in abundance. The Theatrical Owners' Booking Agency (TOBA, known colloquially as Tobytime) had regular venues in the city and touring tent shows played there. Tobytime performers Bessie Smith, Butterbeans and Susie, the Whitman Sisters and Ethel Waters often played in Chicago and were familiar to those who frequented the South Side night haunts. The musical sounds along The Stroll were many and varied. On the corner of the block could be heard the plaintive songs of itinerant blues singers like Blind Blake. In back rooms up in Mecca Flats barrelhouse and boogie pianists strove to improve their unschooled but fertile talents. In dance hall, cabarets and speakeasies all shades of jazz could be heard.

In 1922 at the Lincoln Garden, an eager Louis Armstrong, refreshed after his journey from New Orleans, stepped onto the stage to play with King Oliver and his Creole Jazz Band. 'They was wailin'! I fit right in there sitting with Joe, because I admired him so anyway, y'know? I just went to work. No rehearsal. I know all the guys and I just sat in there and went to work the next night.'

Many fine trumpet players were working in Chicago in 1922. Freddie Keppard was there; so too were Willie Hightower, Joe Sudler, B. T. Wingfield, Tommy Ladnier, Bobby Williams, Jimmy Wade and Bob Shofner. But, as Louis was to state, 'Oliver was *the* man in Chicago, he had the town sewed up.' Richard M. Jones recalled a night when Oliver's old New Orleans rival Keppard turned up at the Lincoln Garden: 'Joe Oliver beat the socks off Keppard...'

On the riverboats, and later in New Orleans, Louis had begun to open up and stretch out on his horn. Stories of his progress had reached Chicago and on one occasion Joe Oliver had visited the riverboats to check Louis out. Baby Dodds who, with his brother John, was playing in the Oliver band recalled:

'Everybody wondered whether he'd let Louis play first or second. Joe said, "It's my band. What am I going to do, play second?" ' Oliver's advice to Louis was, 'Play the melody, play the lead and learn.' Louis played second cornet with the King and continued to learn.

The Oliver band was already a great success in Chicago, but Louis's arrival caused a sensation among musicians. They were fascinated by the improvised cornet breaks of Louis and Joe and regularly crowded into Lincoln Garden just to hear the band. Lil Hardin, playing piano with the band, remembered how white musicians would often come and listen to them. They would listen intently but she couldn't figure out what in particular they were listening to. Drummer George Wettling recalled that Oliver and Louis 'had some breaks they played together that I've never heard played since. I don't know how they knew what was coming up next, but they would play the breaks and never miss.' On the same subject, banjo-playing raconteur Eddie Condon wrote: 'Armstrong seemed able to hear what Oliver was improvising and reproduce it himself at the same time. It seemed impossible so I discounted it, but it was true. Then the two wove around each other like suspicious women talking about the same man.' Muggsy Spanier, recollecting those days, exclaimed, 'Gosh, I wish I could describe the way those two used to play those pretty breaks. Nothing in the world was like it.'

In later years Louis explained how those legendary breaks occurred. 'Whatever he [Oliver] was gonna do, he'd let me know what, four, five bars ahead while the band was jumpin'. Musicians could be sittin' right in front of the bandstand and they couldn't tell when we decided what break we were gonna make ... We weren't readin' any music! I was on to his playin' so well that I just figured my second to it and I'd just go about my business. When the break came it was just there. And the musicians ate it up.'

King Oliver's band was certainly the most popular on the South Side. Louis Metcalf remembered playing opposite the Creole Band at the Lincoln Garden. 'Joe was playing some really great horn—more cornet than Louis. We did a good job, but in our hearts we knew the Oliver band had undressed us.' Harry Dial also felt that, 'As good as Louis was we thought Joe was even greater ... Nobody had the range on the horn that he [Louis] had, nor the ideas but as good as he was, it seemed to us that Joe Oliver had even better ideas and if I can remember, a better tone ... ' Entertainer Tommy Brookins disagreed. 'Armstrong was only rarely heard playing

*King Oliver and his
Creole Jazz
Band—1923.*

solo . . . On that evening when Oliver was sick he played as a member of the ensemble but let Louis solo and, believe me, Louis really played—showing everyone present all he knew, all his tricks, and he received after each song tremendous acclamations.'

At this time Lil Hardin had good reason to remember Louis. 'When Oliver sent for Louis to join him at the Lincoln Garden—I'm at Dreamland, and the second night he's there he brings Louis over to Dreamland to meet me, and I met him while I was playing. I was a little disappointed because all the musicians called Louis "Little Louie", and he weighed 226 pounds! And I said, "Little Louie, wow, Little Louie." ' She asked the other New Orleans boys, 'How come you call him "Little Louie", big as he is? "Well he's been following us around since he was a little boy," they replied.' Lil wasn't impressed. One evening on the bandstand she had her garters rolled down below her knees. 'And he was looking and I said, "This guy's got ideas he'd better not put into words." ' Joe Oliver told Lil, 'You know this Louis, he's a better trumpet player than I'll ever be . . . As long as I keep him playing second to me he won't get ahead of me.' Lil was convinced of the truth of this when at the band's first recording session Louis had to be placed some fifteen feet away from the recording horn so that a balance could be struck between the cornets. Lil began to show more interest in 'Little Louie'.

Lil Hardin came from a respectable and strict family background. When a copy of *St Louis Blues* was found in her possession she was soundly beaten with a broomstick. She learned to play the organ when she was six years old and recalled how she would play for local church services. 'I played *Onward, Christian Soldiers* with a definite beat and the pastor used to look at me over his glasses.' In 1917 Lil moved to Chicago with her mother. One day while Lil was home for the vacation (she studied music for three years at Fisk University), her mother was deeply shocked when her daughter ran back to the house and said that she had been offered a job playing piano in a music store on South State Street. Dicie Hardin was even more scandalized when she later learned that Lil, still a minor, was playing piano at the Deluxe Cafe with the New Orleans Creole Band. After that, Lil 'never got back to the music store—never got back to Fisk University'.

Louis and Lil became very close. 'I commenced to feeling sorry for him but he was good and people were tryin' to keep him back y'know. And that's a bad sign when you start feeling sorry for a man.' Both had been married before; Louis's marriage to Daisy Parker had been precarious from the beginning as was Lil's marriage to Jimmy Johnson, a local cabaret singer. Lil said of Louis, 'He's a fellow who didn't have much confidence in himself to begin with.' Lil, however, had more than enough confidence for both of them and when they decided to marry she organized both her own and Louis's divorce. They were married on 5 February 1924.

Lil had a very friendly personality and was well liked by her fellow musicians but she was a forceful character and very ambitious. She knew what she wanted and it wasn't a 'second trumpet' husband. Preston Jackson said, 'I feel that if it wasn't for Lil, Louis would not be where he is today. She inspired him to do bigger and better things.' Lil felt that Louis deserved more and she told him straight, 'I don't want to be married to a second trumpet player. I want you to play first.' She genuinely believed in Louis's ability. 'When Louis was the only trumpet player he played what he had in himself.' Only Lil could have prised Louis away from Papa Joe and it was her bullying and cajoling that forced the diffident Armstrong to leave the Oliver band and thus begin his meteoric rise to fame. Louis's lack of conviction was wryly recalled by Lil: 'Louis asked, "You made me quit—now what you want me to do?" I said "Just go on out,

Miss Lil.

38

round the musicians, find out who needs a first trumpet-player." '

Jobless, and under orders from Lil, Louis set about the task of finding work, preferably as first trumpet. He approached leading Chicago bandleader Sammy Stewart a light-coloured Negro who turned him down flat. Louis had met with what Earl Hines was to describe as 'blue vein society'. According to Hines it was Louis's blackness which prevented him from getting a job with Stewart and Louis agreed. 'I wasn't up to his society, as a matter of fact I didn't get to play a note for him, he just passed me up and within a few years he could have kicked himself into oblivion, but at the time I could have kicked him.' Stewart was in a minority and, shortly after being turned down, Louis obtained a lead trumpet position with the band of Chicago entertainer Ollie Powers.

Louis's fame was spreading further than the boundaries of Chicago, however, as leading Harlem band leader Sam Wooding explained. 'Armstrong was the man I wanted. He was recognized to be the greatest then, and we sent a wire to make him an offer. I was paying good money for those days, 100 dollars a week and I know I could have shot at Louis. He would have taken it too. Unfortunately I missed him.' Louis had already received a telegram from Wooding's competitor, Fletcher Henderson, inviting him to join his band in New York.

CHAPTER 4

PRINCE OF WAILS

'So when Smack's band hit town and Louis was with them, the guys had never heard anything just like it ... Everyone on the street was talking about the guy.'

Duke Ellington

If the change of scene from balmy New Orleans to the city-slicker sharpness of Chicago's South Side had seemed a big step to Louis, his arrival in New York was cataclysmic. In Chicago he had been greeted by familiar hometown faces and hot music. The impersonal sophistication of musically staid New York stifled him.

The New Orleans message had not taken hold in New York and the jazz was drearily lukewarm. Neither Fletcher 'Smack' Henderson nor his arranger, Don Redman, were yet certain of the genre. Although Henderson's band was very popular, it was strictly a reading unit and followed the dictum of veteran Harlem bandleader J. Tim Brymn: 'The different bands should follow their orchestrations more closely and not try so much of their "ad lib" stuff ... White musicians have excelled coloured players because they are willing to supply novelty music and let it be done by the publisher's arranger, who knows how to do it.'

Louis was to remember his first day in New York, 'I walked up and says, "How do Mr Fletcher. I'm the trumpet player you sent for." All he says is, "Your part's up there." It was *Minnetonka* and that's the first part I played there. I had just left Chicago, where the way we used to do it was just take the wind in, and take what's left of it and blow out—and now I got to watch this part. I was pretty stiff, so they didn't know whether I could play or not ...'

The Henderson band was resident at Roseland, a downtown

ballroom that catered for a white clientele. The band playing opposite Henderson was the slick Sam Lanin outfit.

Initially Louis's problem was his inability to read a score. The Henderson arrangements were much more sophisticated than those of the Marable band. Henderson was to recall many years later: 'In those days he couldn't read music. It was a habit of mine to tell each new musician to follow the score as marked. We were going through a number which had to be played softly and Louis was giving it full blast. We started all over again but Louis was still blowing high. "Louis," I said, "I've already asked you to play it the way it says on the arrangement." I then showed him that the score was marked *pp. Pianissimo*. "Well!" answered Louis, "I thought it meant *pound plenty*!" '

After a week or so, Henderson sent for another musician from Chicago and Louis found it easier to relax. Clarinetist Buster Bailey was an old colleague from Oliver's band. 'I knew Buster could play. So he comes in, and then I kind of had company in the band, and that made a difference. They jumped on *Tiger Rag* I think it was, and they gave me about four choruses— following Buster made me really come on a bit. From then on, I was *in* with the band.'

Smack.
Fletcher Henderson in
1937.

41

Louis's arrival had an amazing effect, not only upon the Henderson band but also upon the relatively pedestrian New York jazz scene in general. Sam Lanin's musicians, hearing Louis from the opposite end of the Roseland Ballroom, came running to see who was 'playing that horn'. When the band performed in Harlem, Louis had exactly the same effect on black musicians. The rhythmic quality which the band developed after Louis's arrival was quite startling and is very obvious on the recordings they made. Trumpet player Bill Coleman remembered hearing Louis on those early Henderson recordings. 'I was hypnotized, paralyzed and knocked out when I heard him.' Cornetist Rex Stewart said, 'I went mad with the rest of the town. I tried to walk like him, talk like him, eat like him, sleep like him. . .'

'The stampeded whites actually deserted house after house and block after block.'
James Weldon Johnson

Between the years 1880 and 1900 Harlem was considered by white middle-class New Yorkers to be a most desirable city suburb. Land plots were eagerly sought and purchased but in the 1904-05, due to over-development, the bottom fell out of the Harlem real estate business. Blacks, trying to improve their living conditions and social standing, took advantage of the market crash and began moving into Harlem, and over the next few years it became an almost totally black community.

1917-18 was a prosperous time for Harlem blacks due mainly to the war in Europe. The urgent need for black workers gave them the opportunity to invest earnings into Harlem real estate. Black fraternal and social organizations sprang up and black-owned enterprises flourished. Simultaneously the seamier side of Harlem life developed: the numbers operation, prostitution and dope peddling. The poorer class couldn't afford exorbitant prices and so apartments were partitioned off and rented. Yet throughout these years and on through the 1920s Harlem was still a prosperous black community with well-lit paved streets and was linked with downtown Manhattan by wide avenues and good public transport.

Black people with talent and creativity gravitated to Harlem: Paul Robeson, Creamer and Layton, Will Marion Cook, Sissle and Blake, Ford Dabney, Williams and Walker, Miller and Lyles, James Reese Europe, James P. Johnson, James Weldon Johnson, Langston Hughes, Florence Mills, Jack Johnson, Will

Vodery, Duke Ellington. The list of artists, writers, musicians, singers and sportsmen is endless and all sought recognition and fame in Harlem.

Between 1900 and 1917 there had been a large influx of mainly classically trained musicians and ragtime pianists seeking employment. Jazz music, although initially deplored by both black and white musical establishments, became increasingly popular and in the 1920s visits to 'Black Harlem' were a white society fad. White Socialites went to hear the jungle music and see the gyrations of the black dancers; to have their bathtub hooch served in teacups by Charleston-stepping black waiters in what they fondly imagined was the black man's natural habitat. Negroes became the vogue but, forever suspicious of the 'ofay' (white), they continued to feel exploited.

Although most of the clubs and dives in Harlem were used by blacks, many were white-owned, as the prohibition era had brought Harlem under the scrutiny of the white crime syndicates. White mobsters regarded the public interest in Harlem as a sound basis for great profit and began investing heavily in nightclubs.

In 1920 the black ex-heavyweight boxing champion Jack Johnson opened the Club DeLuxe. The club failed and Johnson eagerly accepted an offer from the syndicate masterminded by gang boss Owney Madden. Known as Owney the Killer, Madden was one of the most notorious pre-prohibition mobsters in America. The club, re-decorated and re-arranged to maximize seating space, became the most fashionable uptown nightspot in Harlem and was re-named the Cotton Club. A number of 'niteries' became gangster-controlled, among them Small's Paradise, and Connie's Inn which was the hangout of booze racketeer Dutch Schultz. Although featuring black entertainers, they adopted a 'whites only' policy for their clientele.

The two major black theatres in Harlem were the Lafayette and the Lincoln, and some black shows even reached Broadway. The Miller-Lyles-Sissle-Blake show *Shuffle Along* broke the Broadway barrier in 1921 and a section of the white populace became suddenly aware of Negro talent. This interest helped cultivate and finance the 'Harlem Renaissance'.

Louis Armstrong's first visit to New York was short but had far-reaching consequences. Clearly, he affected Henderson's arranger, Don Redman, whose orchestrations had been tentative and undistinguished. To the musical establishment of the day the greatest attribute of the Henderson band was its formal dance band approach. The *Chicago Defender,* a Negro newspaper, said of the pre-Armstrong band that it was 'the greatest, not at all like the average Negro orchestra, but in a class with the good white orchestras, such as Paul Whiteman, Paul Ash and Ted Lewis'. The band sounded 'soft, sweet, and perfect, not the sloppy New Orleans hokum, but peppy blue syncopation'.

The lessons Redman learned from Armstrong's rhythmic, blues-rooted phrasing were to quickly change the sound of the Henderson band. From a poor imitation of a white band, it became a jazz orchestra, and was the foundation of, and major influence upon, the big bands of the early Swing Era.

Drummer Jo Jones said, 'Henderson put class to jazz music . . . His bands largely led to jazz as we have it now.' Armstrong's influence was also felt by others in the band and Coleman Hawkins's tenor saxophone solos suddenly began to take on shape and style.

There were many fine trumpet players in Harlem during this period and all became conscious of Louis: Tom Morris, Pike Davis, Johnny Dunn, Bubber Miley, Ward Pinkett, Louis Metcalf and, perhaps the finest of them all, Joe Smith. A beautifully melodious player, Smith had featured with the Henderson band before Louis's arrival and a certain amount of competition was evident. Louis Metcalf recalled: 'It was a real jazz feud with all the musicians taking sides. It was the most terrific thing I ever heard . . . when Henderson showed off Louis. I don't remember if anybody knew about it in advance, but Joe Smith was sitting in the pit with the house band and, believe me, when he opened the show, it tore the house down. He did five or six encores and probably played better than he ever did before in his life. I guess he did it just to prove that he was still *the* Joe Smith.'

Metcalf recalled that as a result of Smith's performance the management took out part of the show so that Henderson's band could go on right away. 'The first number they played was *Copenhagen*. And Louis's solo was *so* good. But different, and the audience didn't know about how much to applaud. The next number was even better and the people began to dig and were sayin', "Here's another great trumpet player." After the third piece, they really made their minds up. They were sayin', "Now here's another *King*!" And the house was his.' Joe Smith returned later to rejoin the Henderson band and sat in the same section as Louis. What a combination, Louis's hot solos and Joe's beautiful tone. Many years later Louis told Max Jones, 'Joe Smith could do so much with a plunger—made it sound like a human voice.'

Influence was not all one-way traffic. Louis was impressed

Empress of the Blues—Bessie Smith.

by two white trumpet players while he was in New York, both virtuoso performers in white dance orchestras: Vic D'Ippolite, a skilful member of the Sam Lanin trumpet section, and B. A. Rolfe who played with the Vincent Lopez band. Both were brilliant, showy performers. Louis said of Rolfe, 'He would play a tune . . . an octave higher than it was written . . . The way I look at it, that's the way a trumpet *should* play.' He added, 'But I don't dig that skating around a note just because it's high.' Of D'Ippolite he said, 'When it was time to hit the high notes, he hit 'em.' Armstrong's admiration for showy technique had originated with his Waifs' Home training and his own playing on Henderson recordings during this period began to show evidence of the influence. Louis vastly improved his reading skills during his time with Henderson. Henderson himself said, 'He *really* learned to read in my band, and to read in just about every key . . . Louis had to learn, and did learn, much more about his own horn than he knew before he joined us.'

Louis was in great demand in the recording studios during his first stay in New York, mostly as accompanist to the great blues singers of the day. He was superb in this role, providing warm and sensitive backing to Bessie Smith, Clara Smith, Maggie Jones and others. Recalling his sessions with Bessie Smith, he said, 'I remember she just stayed in the studio and wrote the blues there. She finish one, she write another . . . I'm tellin' ya, she used ta just thrill me . . . didn't get to talking to her much, don't think we spoke the same language.' In a BBC interview Max Kaminsky remembered that 'the first time I ever heard Louis he was playing behind Maggie Jones on *Good Time Flat Blues*. My sister used to go round the house singing, "Miss Lizzie Green from New Orleans runs a good time flat"— and that's how I first heard Louis Armstrong. Never forgot that song.'

Louis also recorded for Clarence Williams. The collective personnel employed by Williams included Sidney Bechet and, in contrast to the Henderson recordings of the period, these were in the New Orleans tradition. Williams recorded for two companies, OKeh and Gennett. Lil Armstrong, who was visiting New York at the time, played piano on the Gennett tracks and Clarence Williams himself played on the OKeh sides. Although the band functioned mainly as a backing unit for popular black cabaret singers like Alberta Hunter and Eva Taylor, there was enough space left for individual contributions by the musicians. Both Armstrong and Bechet were able to stretch out and feature magnificently in the ensembles.

However, Louis was becoming increasingly disenchanted with the Henderson band. The sidemen were notoriously casual and Henderson was slack with discipline. Louis later admitted that he did not approve of the careless attitudes within the band. He was always totally dedicated to his work and expected others to be equally serious. He knew what his life might have been. The respect and admiration showered on him were due entirely to his music, and it would always remain the most important thing in his life.

Meanwhile, in Chicago, Lil was becoming increasingly impatient for Louis's return. On her visit to New York she had taken due note that Louis was not given billing with the Henderson band. Also there was talk linking Louis with a New York chorus girl. Lil talked Bill Bottoms into booking her into Dreamland, telling him that she would be bringing her husband back from New York to front the band. She also insisted that Dreamland should bill him as *Louis Armstrong: The World's Greatest Trumpet Player*. How she managed to persuade Bottoms to agree will never be known, but agree he did and Lil sent a telegram to Louis telling him to return to Chicago, 'I got a job for you for 75 dollars a week.' Louis didn't believe her: 'He wasn't anxious to become a star . . . So I said: "Well I've already got the job and if you're not here, don't come at all" . . . So then he came . . . he said "What do you mean calling me the World's Greatest Trumpet Player? And I betcha I don't get 75 dollars a week." I said: "I bet you do." So I got the contract and showed it to him and he said, "Well I still think you're crazy." '

Before he left New York, Louis tried to persuade the young Rex Stewart to take his place in the Henderson band. Rex remembered, 'In the normal circumstances I'd have taken a job with that band even if the money had been less than I was getting . . . But I wasn't keen to follow Louis Armstrong.' Stewart did eventually join Henderson while Louis, now back in Chicago, began the most important period of his career.

By 1925 bitter jealousies and violent confrontations of early prohibition days in Chicago had reached a critical point. Dion O'Banion, the psychopathic boss of the Irish-Jewish North Side faction, was shot dead at his flower shop. O'Banion's antagonist Al Capone commented laconically, 'O'Banion's head got away from his hat.' Battle forces gathered in the fight for supreme control over illegal booze and crime in the city. O'Banion was succeeded by Hymie Weiss. Then Johnny Torrio, Capone's boss, was shot and wounded near his house by Bugs Moran, one of Weiss's cohorts. Chastened and afraid, Torrio relinquished his

46

grip and was jailed. Later he was released and fled to New York where he joined forces with Lucky Luciano. Without Torrio's experience Capone was temporarily disadvantaged but gradually he gained the upper hand. His rise culminated in the St Valentine's Day Massacre of 1929.

Gang warfare regularly encroached upon the working lives of jazz musicians. Muggsy Spanier told how he saw two men shot to death in front of him. 'Keep playing' was the maxim in those days, and Spanier did just that, although afterwards he could not remember the tune and was so saturated with nervous sweat that he had to change his clothes—including his shoes. Capone himself was renowned for his big tips and often visited the clubs to hear jazz music. As one mobster told Spanier, 'Jazz has got guts, it don't make you slobber.' Mezz Mezzrow was one musician who disapproved of the uneasy alliance between jazz and the mob. 'It was all one great big underworld and they'd put their dirty grabbers on the one good thing left on earth, our music, and sucked it down into the mud with them.' Cornet player Jimmy McPartland remembered a night when one gang turned over a rival club. 'The mobsters would break a bottle over some guy's head, jab it in his face, then maybe kick him. They made mincemeat of people. I never saw such a horrible thing in my life. But we kept on playing—period. A couple more nights of work and they came and did it again, much worse.' Police raids became so commonplace that Earl Hines 'stood up in the wagon so often on these trips, I finally decided to *run* and get a seat when the police came.' As Louis Armstrong succinctly commented, 'Danger was dancing all around you back then.'

Louis was relatively unaffected by the violence that surrounded him. He did not consider it unusual, nor was he overly excited by such behaviour. He had, after all, grown up with such dangers. As a youth in New Orleans he worked in Sicilian-owned' tonks and learned to keep his mind on his own business. Zutty Singleton remembered Louis's matter-of-fact presence of mind in one dangerous situation. A gangster was slapping a girl around in front of the stage 'and came up with a big pistol and asked Louis did he like it or not. And Louis said, "That's all right with me." ' Another time when the bullets began to fly Louis was the only one who didn't duck; 'he just kept playing'. For Louis it was just part of a night's work—all of which there was plenty. 'Things were jumping so around Chicago at that time, there was more work than a cat could shake a stick at.'

Louis's return to Chicago was a triumph. He was now master

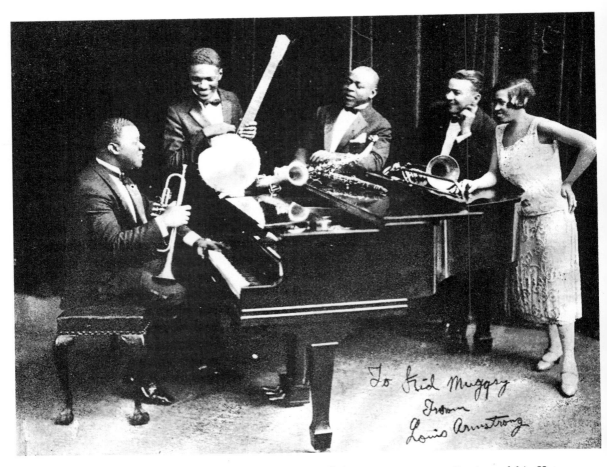

To Kid Muggsy from Louis Armstrong

Louis and his Hot Five—1926.
Louis, Johnny St Cyr, Johnny Dodds, Kid Ory, Lil Armstrong.

of his instrument and within the next two to three years was to advance jazz playing beyond the reach of many of his New Orleans colleagues. Musicians crowded Dreamland to hear Louis with Lil Armstrong's eight-piece band. Louis recalled, 'She had a damned good band.' Very soon it was not only musicians who came crowding in; everyone in Chicago wanted to hear Louis. Edward M. Reeves was a member of these audiences. 'Cheek-by-jowl, we sat, danced, and listened. Gangsters, stockbrokers, university students, visiting musicians, men with no visible means of support. Ladies of the evening, squares, slumming suburbanites, and a fringe of people from the sight-seeing buses, came to see and hear the Devil in his den ... All this and fifteen choruses of *Tiger Rag*, from Louis's golden horn ...' Lil remembered how 'they'd line up ten deep at the Dreamland ... Mostly white fellows would line up in front of the stand.' Louis began 'doubling up', working at the Vendome Theatre with Erskine Tate's fifteen-piece orchestra. Before going to New York, working with the Tate

48

band with its repertoire of overtures and classics would have presented Louis with problems, but his time with Henderson had been profitable and he now was a rounded musician well able to cope with Tate's book.

His work at the Vendome brought Louis to the attention of an even wider audience. It was reported that people would often visit the theatre for Louis's performance only, and leave before the film was shown. Louis said, 'I learned a lot playing under the direction of Erskine Tate, we played all kinds of music. I really did sharpen up on my reading there . . . I got a solo on stage, and my big thing was *Cavalleria Rusticana.*' Trumpet player Doc Cheatham remembered substituting for Louis once at the Vendome. Cheatham had to play a solo on *Poor Little Rich Girl.* He recalled that as the spotlight fell on him 'people began screaming, then as I soloed they just went right down when they realized it wasn't Louis. That hurt me most of all.'

The music critic for the *Chicago Defender,* Dave Peyton (himself a bandleader), wrote, 'Louis Armstrong, the greatest cornet player in the country, is drawing many "ofay" [white] musicians to Dreamland nightly, to hear him blast out those weird jazz figures. This boy is in a class by himself.' As is always the case when a champion surfaces there were many contenders for his crown. Peyton himself was not beyond testing Armstrong's skills. He led the resident pit band at the Regal Theatre. One night, knowing that Louis was shortly to appear on stage, he arranged to feature his trumpet star, Reuben Reeves, who was a well-schooled expert musician. Danny Barker recalls in his autobiography how Louis, hearing Reeves's pyrotechnics, peeped through the curtain and watched Peyton directing Reeves and was stung by this deliberate act of sabotage. Barker records how Louis eventually went on stage and blew 'one or two hundred choruses of *Chinatown . . .* Reeves and Peyton sat petrified.'

Many such incidents have been recorded. Lil Armstrong recalled one night at Dreamland when Freddie Keppard came along to best Louis and said to him, ' "Boy, let me have your trumpet." So, Freddie blew—oh, he blew and he blew and he blew and then the people gave him a nice hand. Then he handed the trumpet back to Louis. And I said, "Now get him, get him!" Ooh, never in my life have I heard such trumpet playing! If you want to hear Louis play, just hear him play when he's *angry.*' Earl Hines told Stanley Dance of an occasion when Johnny Dunn was in town with a visiting show and showed up at the Sunset Cafe. 'Johnny went out on the floor and, boy, he was blowing! He had people with him from the theatre, and he was known about Chicago . . . After he got through playing the blues he handed Louis's horn back . . . Nobody said this was a cutting contest, that Louis was going to try to outplay this man . . . when it came to Louis's turn I don't know how many choruses he played, but every time he played a new one he just kept getting higher and higher. That was the end of the trumpet for that night . . .'

King Oliver also dropped in occasionally when Louis was at the Sunset Cafe but when he sat in the competition was always on a friendly basis. Wild Bill Davison remembered Oliver joining Armstrong one night. '125 choruses of *Tiger Rag*— exchanging choruses. People went insane . . .'

Punch Miller, a very fine trumpet player from New Orleans who has received less credit than he deserves due mainly to his own wanderlust, was in Chicago at the time. Miller preferred touring with shows and circuses rather than establishing himself in any of the entertainment centres of America. Consequently he made very few recordings during the 1920s. The sides he did make, with Tiny Parham, Albert Wynn and Frankie 'Half Pint' Jaxon, show him to be an exciting player with a driving, sparkling style. Although an excellent 'head' player he was, along with many other good trumpet men like Doc Cheatham, Guy Kelly, George Mitchell and Reuben Reeves, less than a match for Louis.

One trumpet player who had the wherewithal to cover Louis was Jabbo Smith. Jabbo came from a similar background to Louis and had gained his early training in an orphanage band. He was sensationally fast, as Milt Hinton told Stanley Dance: 'He could play so very soft, but he was also the first I heard to play fast, fluid trumpet . . . Jabbo didn't make a feature of high notes, but he played high, and he had full mastery of his horn from top to bottom.' Hinton described how Jabbo played 'rapid-fire passages while Louis was melodic and beautiful'. Whenever they met in cutting contests it was always a close thing but Hinton confirmed, 'It's true that Louis was the greatest soloist.'

After the Dreamland job folded, Louis joined Carroll Dickerson at the Sunset Cafe. Recalling those days, Bud Freeman commented, 'Louis would play twenty or more improvised choruses, always to an exciting climax.' The Dickerson band had Earl Hines playing piano, and in Hines Louis found a musician of his own calibre. Together they made an extraordinarily fine musical partnership which culminated in some superb recordings. Although both Louis and Hines had established personal styles before they met, both musicians

Jabbo remembering the 1920s.
Jabbo Smith—1983.

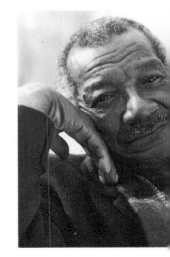

50

Louis Armstrong's Sunset Cafe Stompers—1927. Earl Hines did much of the leading as the photo suggests.

were to gain much from each other.

While at the Sunset, Louis provided musical support for many cabaret acts. In particular he was noticed for the way he emphasized the movements of the Brown and McGraw tap-dancing team. Louis himself also began to perform on the cabaret floor. At first he was a rather uncertain partner to the experienced and popular Chicago entertainer, Mae Alix. Earl Hines described to Stanley Dance how Alix, who knew Louis was timid, would take advantage of him. 'She would throw her arms around his neck and sing, "I need a Big Butter and Egg Man." He would stand there and almost melt . . . and the whole house cracked up.' But Louis, intent on learning his craft, was soon a master of this new facet of his career and it was not long before he became an exuberant entertainer. 'Percy Venables, the producer of the show, staged a finale with four of us band boys closing the show doing the Charleston. That was really something. There was Earl Hines, as tall as he was; Tubby Hall, as fat as he was; Little Joe Walker, as short as he is; and myself, as fat as I was at that time. We would stretch out across that floor doing the Charleston as fast as the music would play it. Boy, oh boy, you talking about four cats picking them up and laying them down—that was us . . .'

Louis always remembered his time in Chicago as the finest of his life, 'I spent my youngest and best days there.' He and Zutty Singleton, his friend from New Orleans, played for a time in the Clarence Jones Orchestra at the Metropole Theatre. Zutty, Louis and Earl Hines became fast friends and went everywhere together. Earl Hines, reminiscing about those years, recalled, 'Louis was wild and I was wild, and we were inseparable. He was the most happy-go-lucky guy I ever met.' Charlie Carpenter remembered, 'After the Sunset, Louis, Earl and Zutty Singleton had made a pact not to work unless all three were hired.' The three friends tried to stay together as one unit and at one period opened their own club. Without backing, the venture proved disastrous. Hines recalled, 'I don't know what happened but we like to starve to death, making a dollar or a dollar-and-a-half apiece a night. So we drifted apart . . .' Louis and Zutty went to work at the Savoy Ballroom and an aggrieved Hines asked, 'What you doing to me?' Louis explained, 'It's rough out here, I gotta make them payments on the house . . . We tried to talk you in . . .'

In 1928 Louis and the Dickerson band began broadcasting regularly from Chicago's Savoy Ballroom, airshots that brought Louis increased popularity. With his recording groups he continued making splendid recordings throughout this period. Although still under contract to OKeh, he did some occasional moonlighting. On one occasion, in 1926, Louis made two sides for Vocalion under the name of Lil's Hot Shots. A displeased OKeh executive hauled Louis into the office. Playing the record over, he asked Louis who he thought was singing. Louis replied, 'I don't know but I won't do it again.'

The Hot Five and Hot Seven recordings made between 1925 and 1929 are among the greatest and most important recordings in jazz. Louis's development over the period can be heard clearly and his swift domination over the conventional New Orleans ensemble can be charted: from such 1925 recordings as *Gut Bucket Blues* through early virtuoso displays on *Cornet Chop Suey* in 1926 to masterworks like *Potato Head Blues* in 1927 and the technical triumphs of the Armstrong-Hines duet on *Weatherbird* in 1928. Before Hines exerted his influence Louis had been ably supported by Johnny Dodds, the greatest of blues clarinet players. One record on which Dodds was featured caused quite a stir in Chicago. This was *Heebie Jeebies,* and during the recording Louis allegedly forgot the words and started scatting. Some indication of the effect this recording had can be gauged from Mezz Mezzrow's comments. *'Heebie Jeebies . . .* This record of Louis's took all of Chicago by storm

. . . For months after that you would hear cats greeting each other with Louis riffs when they met around town—"I got the heebies, I got the jeebies" and the next minute they were scatting in each other's face. Louis's recordings almost drove the English language out of the Windy City for good.' The record was also a favourite of Bix Beiderbecke, as Mezzrow recalled: '. . . we grabbed those cats out of their pads and played *Heebie Jeebies* for them, they all fractured their wigs . . . Bix kept chuckling as the record played over . . . He never did get over that masterpiece.' Something of the impact that the Hot Five and Seven recordings had on musicians can be judged by a story told by Wingy Manone. 'We used to play platters . . . by Louis. Jack [Teagarden] . . . was gone on . . . a tune called *Oriental Strut* . . . Jack thought that was the end. He decided nobody else could ever top that, and said we ought to put it away someplace to preserve it for posterity . . . Jack and I drove out on the mesa with it. We dug a big hole and laid that record away, and as far as I know it is still there today.'

An interesting recording made by Louis in 1927 is *Chicago Breakdown*. Instead of the usual pickup group, Louis fronts the Dickerson band, which played regularly at the Sunset Cafe. Other examples of working bands of that period are the Erskine Tate Vendome Theatre orchestra's coupling of *Static Strut* and *Stomp Off, Let's Go* and two sides, *Symphonic Raps* and *Savoyagers Stomp*, recorded in 1928 with Dickerson's Savoy Ballroom band. (A detailed discussion of Louis's recordings appears in Chapter 9.)

The 'Black and Tan' night spots in Chicago allowed blacks and whites to mix freely, and Wingy Manone would often join Louis during their free hours (something they could not easily have done in their native New Orleans). Wingy recalled, 'Louis took us [Manone and pianist Art Hodes] to an after-hours rib joint. It was a barbeque place and in those days the rats ran all around them places. Louis told the woman who owned the joint "Baby bring me and my friends each a big batch of that barbeque that the rats have run on." ' Wingy also introduced Max Kaminsky to Louis. Many years afterwards Kaminsky could still detail his feelings at that first meeting. 'When Louis came over to the table . . . I was introduced to him. From listening to his records I already had some inkling of the warmth and power of the man, but I was totally unprepared for that remarkable penetrating awareness underneath the genial, easy going manner. All his senses seem to receive impressions of you; you feel he's not so much sizing you up as opening his mind to you, like a receiving set. You can't fake it with Louis. He can tell.' Kaminsky was equally overwhelmed by Louis's playing. 'I was just unprepared for the full impact of his playing . . . he broke the place up. He broke me up, too . . . the combination of Louis's dazzling virtuosity and sensational brilliance of tone so overwhelmed me that I felt as if I had stared into the sun's eye . . .'

In 1927 the Melrose Music Company transcribed some Armstrong breaks and solos. They were issued in book form as *125 Jazz Breaks for Cornet* and *50 Hot Choruses for Cornet*, and over the years trumpet players all over the world have benefited from these transcriptions.

In 1929 Tommy Rockwell of OKeh Records suggested to Louis that he should return to New York. Rockwell, who wished to become Louis's manager, intended that the trumpeter should go alone but presumably Louis was not aware of this. The Dickerson band was a close-knit group and decided to stick together and accompany Louis to the Big Apple. So, in a number of dilapidated vehicles, the full band set out to conquer New York. Zutty Singleton recounted how they 'loaded all the stuff into the car. Finally Lil made a loan on something and got 25 dollars for each of us. That was some trip.'

'The Great Depression was the most persuasive, the most persistent and the most destructive economic crisis the nation had ever faced.'
                                                          Cabell Phillips

---

The stock market crash of 1929 sent a chain reaction shivering through America. The national economy took a nose dive, sliding downhill at an alarming rate. The resulting depression touched every section of industry and commerce. Social barriers were tossed aside as suffering and distress indiscriminately affected millions. Perhaps the worst hurt were those who were least familiar to hardship. The middle class felt suddenly degraded, the working class lived insecure lives at the best of times. Inevitably, the black community suffered most.

Black poet Langston Hughes commented cynically, 'The depression brought everyone down a peg or two and the Negro had few pegs to fall.'

Breadlines and soup kitchens became an everyday reality for a quarter of the nation's workforce. The jobless clustered around street corners, in community parks and poolrooms; hobo jungles sprang up at every freight terminal as men dispersed aimlessly across the country.

In downtown Manhattan, theatres and clubs closed down but in Harlem they struggled to keep doors open. At the Savoy Ballroom and at the Lafayette Theatre, where they kept on swingin', it was business as usual.

Louis and the Dickerson band arrived in New York penniless. When the only car to survive the journey arrived in 42nd Street the radiator boiled over and 'a cop came over and searched for shotguns 'cause he'd seen the Chicago licence plates'. Rockwell was somewhat aggrieved when he realized that Louis had not come alone but managed to obtain work for the band and, after a spell at the Savoy Ballroom in Harlem, booked them into a

Louis and the Carroll Dickerson band—1929.

four-month residency at Connie's Inn. Max Kaminsky remembered, 'To hear Louis Armstrong swing the floor show at Connie's Inn in 1929 was *really* something. He'd get that chorus line of shapely young sepia-skinned girls stepping high, wide, and I mean hot.'

Louis was in great demand. Ralph J. Gleason tells how he 'played downtown in the Hudson Theatre for a show with the *Connie's Inn Hot Chocolate Revue*. Then he went uptown at midnight for a late show at the Lafayette Theatre in Harlem and after that played a breakfast set at the Connie's Inn

Cabaret!' In the *Hot Chocolate* show at the Hudson, where Louis was backed by the Leroy Smith Orchestra, the main feature was the Waller-Razaf number *Ain't Misbehavin'*, and at each performance it stole the show. Nevertheless, there were still those who felt confident enough to vie with Louis. Rudy Powell remembered such a battle taking place at the Savoy Ballroom where Rex Stewart was appearing with the Benny Carter band. The trumpet battle started at the Savoy and later continued at the Lenox Club. By the time they reached the club 'Rex had blown himself out. Louis was well aware of the situation but he was not one to let a challenger off easily. He added insult to injury by playing *When You're Smiling* an octave higher than his tops at the time. Rex was so disgusted, he broke all the water glasses on the bandstand.'

The effect Louis had on Harlem was tremendous. In his autobiography Mezz Mezzrow described how he managed to persuade the boss of a juke box company to put Louis's recording of *Ain't Misbehavin'* on his machines. It proved so successful that soon they used all Louis's recordings immediately on their release. 'They all hit the juke boxes and they rocked all Harlem.'

Louis was a success with white audiences and this was cause for justifiable pride among the black community. Few members of their race had ever made such an impression on 'white time' before. Mezzrow described how Louis's habit of holding a white handkerchief in his hand and clasping his hands in front of himself became a craze in Harlem. 'Pretty soon all the kids were hanging around "The Corner" with their hands locked in front of them and a white handkerchief always peeking out from between their fingers. . . . All the raggedy kids . . . were so inspired with self-respect after digging how neat and natty Louis was, they started to dress up real good, and took pride in it too, because if Louis did it, it must be right.'

In back alleys behind the theatres and clubs in Harlem those who hadn't the price of entry would listen at stage doors. Mezzrow described it thus: '. . . the sidewalk was covered with snow, so we'd run into the alleyway and huddle up in front of a large exhaust fan . . . You could hear Louis . . . if you didn't choke first on the smoke and funk that was pumped in your face . . . Roaches [marijuana] were passed round and round and even though some of those vipers were plenty raggedy they loved Louis like nobody else. We spent most all the winter of 1930 squoze together in front of that fan shed.'

During this period (1929-30) Louis was at the height of his creative powers. His recordings show his prodigious talent at its very peak. In his biography of Armstrong, James Lincoln

Collier describes this period as 'the fork in the road'. Collier writes, 'On one hand, there was a potentially large audience out there waiting for him, drawn to his mugging, his stage personality. On the other hand there was jazz, recognized as a music worthy of respect by many intellectuals, musicians, ordinary fans.' Collier's words imply that Louis gave conscious consideration to a choice between general popularity or jazz immortality. However, it is unlikely that Louis ever saw his career in these terms. The gradual build-up, first of learning to play his horn, then the realization that his prowess was second to none and, finally, the speedily learned ablity to hold an audience with comic asides and stage presence, were considered by Louis as one. There was no division—he was a born extrovert, an entertainer. When Tommy Rockwell offered to guide his career to great commercial success as a solo performer, any hesitancy on Louis's part was with regard to old friendships, not artistic integrity.

Louis did not differentiate between artistic merit and entertainment. If what he did was considered art, then that was okay just as long as it didn't interfere with business.

Clarinetist Joe Muranyi, who played with Louis near the end of his career, recalled in a filmed interview for the BBC an incident when a band member was drunk and fouled up a performance. Louis turned on the hapless individual and hissed, 'Don't fuck with my hustle.' That was how Louis saw his illustrious career: he loved his music and was proud of it but it was all hustle. Burt Korall summed it up neatly: 'Armstrong merely continued to be Armstrong, bringing his talent to bear on pop material, enlarging and enlivening and enriching it, making many of the songs unforgettable. Some of the material continues to exist today only because Pops put his mark on it!' Trumpet player Jimmy Maxwell was in full agreement: 'In the 1930s Louis just kept on getting better . . . Pop material? Louis had to get into it. Where else was there to go? And what he did with it!' What indeed! Who would ever expect to remember *When It's Sleepy Time Down South* if not for Louis?

Tommy Rockwell managed Louis in the early 1930s and had a considerable effect on his career, as he was also to have on a number of major talents in the 1930s. Although he had only a modicum of taste, Rockwell did have the knack of knowing what the public would go for. He must be credited with guiding Louis away from Race and jazz material to good quality popular songs by first-rate tunesmiths like Hoagy Carmichael and Fats Waller and his lyricist Andy Razaf. This change of emphasis was an important innovation and was to benefit all jazz stylists

immeasurably. Such popular tunes as *Stardust, I'm Confessin',*
Body and Soul and *If I Could Be With You (One Hour Tonight)*
became standard jazz vehicles and ultimately helped entice
many more listeners into the jazz fold.

In their definitive record of Louis's career, Max Jones and
John Chilton point out that during the Depression years public
taste was geared towards such sweet sounds as the Guy
Lombardo Orchestra and to crooners like Bing Crosby. If Louis
had not changed his repertoire he would surely have sunk into
an obscurity like that which enveloped so many jazz artists of
the 1920s. As it was, Louis worked continuously through the
Depression years. He rarely had long residencies, as in the
Chicago days, but toured the country playing mainly one night
stands. It was tough going. Trombonist J.C. Higginbotham, who
played in Louis's band during the 1930s, remembered touring
with Louis in the South for five days and nights without sleep.
Some of the bands Louis fronted were not the best and Zutty
Singleton asked him, 'How can you play with such a band?'
Louis replied, 'I don't even hear them.' In a letter to Luis Russell
during this period Louis wrote, 'Come out here and play for me
because these . . . cats can't swing that old New Orleans jive.'

Critics have condemned Louis's work in the 1930s but
musicians continued to idolize him. Trombonist Lawrence
Brown recalled how 'Every trumpet player at that time tried
to play *one* of his choruses.' Cat Anderson agreed. 'We played
all Louis Armstrong's things note for note.' Buck Clayton
remembered walking down a street in Los Angeles in 1931 and
hearing an Armstrong record playing. 'It was *I'm Confessin'*
and I just stopped right there and listened. I wouldn't walk any
further, because it was such a beautiful interpretation . . . how
pretty it was. I admired that record so much—not so much for
execution . . . which he was known to have, but just for the
beauty of it.'

Harry Dial, relating how he joined Louis's band as a
drummer in 1933, thought the band sounded 'really putrid'.
Dial was under the illusion that Louis could not play anymore
but soon lost that opinion. 'We used to get out in those little
towns in the mid-West where people didn't know him too well
. . . so he'd sit down and really play horn . . . He'd play *High
Society* and *Tiger Rag* which used to work the stew out of any
drummer because he'd never stop where he'd say he was going
to . . . He'd hit as many as 350 high Cs on *Shine.* I used to count
them. He'd make me so mad on *Tiger Rag* that I wouldn't know
what to do. He'd want me to ride the cymbals on the last three
choruses . . . I'd grab the cymbal around the 8th chorus and

start riding it . . . and by the end of the 10th it would sound good to him and . . . he'd hit with one finger, which would mean one more chorus, and I'd ride it again . . . the end of the 11th . . . and he'd play ten more choruses. I used to go in to work sharp as a tack, groomed all down and by the time I'd finish the first set I used to look like a bum, my collar was all down, my feet were wet, and my suit looked like I slept in it. That guy worked me to death . . . He told me . . . "I'm only playing by the bass, drums and piano. I ain't paying those other guys no mind." He used to tell Teddy [Wilson], "I don't want any of that fancy stuff on the piano, I want to hear those changes." '

Roy Eldridge, who would be a major innovator himself a few years later, saw Louis at New York's Lafayette Theatre in 1932. 'I was a young cat, and I was very fast, but I wasn't telling no

Zutty Singleton.

59

kind of story . . . He started out like a new book, building and building, chorus after chorus, and finally reaching a full climax, ending on his high F. It was a real climax, right, clean, clear. The rhythm was rocking, and he had that sound going along. . . . He was building the thing all the time instead of just playing in a straight line.'

Louis's work during the 1930s has often been discounted as commercial hokum. Jazz critics wildly overreacted in condemning his output during those years. Tommy Rockwell saw the band's function as a bolster for Louis's extraordinary talent rather than a collective unit such as the Henderson or Ellington band. Armstrong's talent was so immense that little room was left for other soloists. Only occasional forays, by trombone, clarinet or saxophone for contrast, were felt to be necessary. The Dickerson band was a good accompanying unit for Louis, but Rockwell felt that he should dispense with it and Louis reluctantly agreed, thereby causing considerable ill feeling, particularly with Zutty Singleton. Singleton remembered asking Louis if he wanted him to stay with him 'Because if not I've got a job to stay in Connie's Inn. And so Louis told me how much money he had a chance to make and everything like that. And that's when I told Louis, I said, "Well, Louis, friendship is one thing and business is another." '

The bands that Louis used after the split with Dickerson were not always of the best, their recorded output is uneven and occasionally they stand accused of playing out of tune. This was mainly due to lack of preparation, but critics have overemphasized this fact and in so doing have caused unwarranted neglect to some of Louis's finest masterpieces— not to mention some good big band accompaniment.

It is worth noting that many musicians, including such dissimilar trumpet stylists as Bobby Hackett and Maynard Ferguson, have mentioned that *Struttin' with Some Barbeque* was their first choice among Louis's recordings—not the Hot Five version of 1927, an accepted classic, but the 1935 recording with the Luis Russell band (and this despite an unscored and ill-conceived clarinet solo by Bingie Madison). Louis's solo on this number is glorious and anything other than the big-band backdrop would surely have been inappropriate.

Louis had his greatest influence on other musicians during the early 1930s. He was commercial but, far from diminishing the jazz content of his performance, he showed himself to be the trumpet man of his time with more fire, soul, inspiration and technique, not to mention tone, than any of his contemporaries. Listening to Jabbo Smith's recordings of 1929

60

we can enthuse over his imagination and superb technique, but listen afterwards to an Armstrong record from the same period and immediately Smith is overshadowed. Louis's inspired tone and solo buildup are incomparable.

In 1930, without a regular group, Louis guested with the Luis Russell band for a number of theatre dates and played a two-month season with the Mills Blue Rhythm Band. He recorded with both bands but in July of that year he decided to accept a booking on the West Coast.

CHAPTER 5

STARDUST

'Louis's engagements in California were at Sebastian's Cotton Club in Culver City...If one had to pick a dozen consecutive sides to depict Louis's amazing consistency they would be the twelve from this period.'
John Chilton

The film industry began moving to Southern California around 1907. The rainy season and regular sunshine were ideal for an industry perpetually hampered in the East with problems of winter shooting. Producers began sending small companies out to Los Angeles and gradually the necessary facilities were established. By 1918 most major companies had a studio on the West Coast.

In those early days Los Angeles was a cluster of small but ever-increasing communities surrounded by a wilderness of briar and bramble-covered dunes. By 1926 the Hollywood community was a thriving factory town of film folk and as the film industry expanded so did the demand for sophisticated socializing.

In 1927 Frank Sebastian bought the Green Mill Club, which was situated just across from the MGM lot. After redecoration Sebastian opened his new club, now calling it Sebastian's New Cotton Club. In a city where night spots proliferated, the New Cotton Club was noted for lavish shows, glittering entertainment and hot music. Situated where it was, the club's clientele was liberally sprinkled with famous movie stars. The choice of Louis Armstrong as chief attraction in 1930 could not have been better timed. He was an immediate success.

California has a very reputable jazz history going back to around 1917 when Jelly Roll Morton first arrived in Los Angeles. Morton, that most brashly self-confident of men, had no difficulty fitting in. 'People thought it was strange that I had come to Los Angeles with only one suit...of course, after my trunks got there, I turned the town out. They thought I was one of the movie stars.' In 1921 both the Kid Ory and King Oliver bands worked in the area. In their biography of King Oliver, Rust and Allen refer to a West Coast band organized by Morton which had in its trumpet section Oliver, Mutt Carey and King Porter.

One of the early influential figures on the West Coast was Reb Spikes who, along with his brother John, was involved in many facets of the entertainment business. Spikes owned a touring company and also worked as a booking agent. A musician himself, Spikes was billed as the 'World's Greatest Saxophonist' and as such he toured the territory with a number of minstrel shows. In 1920 Spikes was leading his own 'So-Different Orchestra' to considerable local acclaim. His band included, at various times, trumpeter George Orendorff, saxophonist Les Hite, and clarinetist Jimmy Strong, all of whom were later to play with Louis Armstrong. Always a businessman, Reb Spikes was the first entrepreneur to import Race records to the West Coast and he eventually formed his own recording company. It was this last action that earned Spikes a lasting place in jazz history. In 1921 the recordings he made of the Kid Ory band were the first to be made by a coloured jazz band.

'Good taste is good business'

Will H. Hays

When Louis Armstrong arrived in Los Angeles in 1930 to front the New Cotton Club house band, the glamorous and unreal aspects of early Hollywood cinema were being superceded by a new realism typified by the gangster movies of that era. Gang warfare was still rife in city streets and prohibition an ever-increasing absurdity.

Darryl F. Zanuck, head of production at Warner Brothers, sensed that Great Depression audiences were in no mood for the romanticism of earlier Hollywood productions. Included in that year's film releases were *Little Caesar* starring Edward G. Robinson, and *The Public Enemy* featuring James Cagney, both of which remain classics of the genre.

Despite individual box office successes, it is probable that the only film companies to make money in the depressed years 1930-31 were Walt Disney and MGM. At the height of the Depression, audiences could often be enticed into the cinema

Louis and the New Cotton Club orchestra in Culver City—1930.

only by the promise of a second feature comedy and a Mickey Mouse cartoon. MGM's epic for 1930 was *Trader Horn*. Over at Paramount was the new sensation, Marlene Dietrich, working on her current role of Shanghai Lil in Zukor's *Shanghai Express*. Meanwhile, Maurice Chevalier and Jeanette MacDonald were warbling their way through *One Hour with You*.

Universal already had a box-office success with *All Quiet on the Western Front*, and at the Fox studios work was beginning on *Scarface*, which was to feature Paul Muni. Modelled on the career of Al Capone, the film depicted the St Valentine's Day Massacre of 1929 and the murder of Legs Diamond. It was to be the last of the major gangster films of that period; by 1932 they had all but disappeared from the screens as the 'dictator of screen virtue' Will H. Hays reacted to a storm of disapproval emanating from the Daughters of the American Revolution and the American Legion. Hays might well have done better for the industry if, rather than condemn those films that basically moralized against crime, he had reflected upon such real violence as that which went on behind the cameras on the Paramount lot. There, director Norman Taurog was terrorizing his ten-year-old nephew Jackie Cooper on the set of *Skippy*, a film based on a heartwarming comic-strip character. The petrified Cooper was ordered to cry for one scene by his uncle who threatened to kill the child's dog if he did not oblige. Not unnaturally, Cooper cried, and the film became immensely popular — even having a brand of peanut butter named after the principal character.

'When I saw Pops for the first time he was going to a rehearsal at Frank Sebastian's Cotton Club . . . he looked pretty sharp. His hair looked nice and shiny and he had on a pretty grey suit. He wore a tie that looked like an ascot tie with an extra-big knot in it. Soon all the hip cats were wearing big knots in their ties. We called them Louis Armstrong knots.

Buck Clayton

Louis's stay in Los Angeles was short, successful and traumatic. A great success at the club and on the radio link-up that the club had, he also made his first appearance on-screen in a film entitled *Ex-Flame*. Louis made some of his most exciting records while on the West Coast, among them *Body and Soul*, *I'm a Ding Dong Daddy*, *Confessin'*, *Sweethearts on Parade* and *Just a Gigolo*. On the debit side was his arrest, along with white drummer Vic Berton, for possessing marijuana.

Louis had started smoking marijuana in Chicago. Lyricist Charles Carpenter recalled being back stage at the Savoy Ballroom when a white arranger told Louis, 'I got a new cigarette, man. It makes you feel good.' After a while Louis said, 'Let me try it.' Later, Mezz Mezzrow became his chief supplier. Louis's version of his arrest in Los Angeles is well recorded by Jones and Chilton. 'It was during our intermission at this big night club which was packed and jammed every night with all sorts of my fans, including movie stars. Anyway, while Vic and I were blasting this joint — having lots of laughs and feeling good . . . we were standing in this great big lot in front of some cars. Just then two big healthy Dicks [detectives] came from behind a car — nonchalantly — and said to us, "We'll take the roach, boys." '

Vic Berton's brother Ralph takes up the story: 'The cops took

Vic and Louis downtown where they spent the night in a cell laughing it up – they were still high. They stopped laughing the next morning, when the judge gave them six months and one thousand dollars fine each.'

With the help of Frank Sebastian and Tommy Rockwell, Louis had his sentence suspended and was soon back at the Club blowing for his fans. Although shaken by the incident, he continued to use marijuana for the rest of his life. Shortly afterwards, Louis returned to Chicago where he formed another band.

His return was triumphant. He and his new band were booked to appear at the Regal Theatre by Johnny Collins, who had become his manager. How Collins came to take control of Louis's career is uncertain. Budd Johnson thought that Collins was a lawyer. 'When Louis was jailed on the marijuana charge, Rockwell sent Collins out to get him out of jail but somehow Collins and his wife snatched Louis away from them.'

Trouble, however, continued to dog him. 'In Chicago all I wanted was a little elbow room. Every time you looked around it seemed there was a gun in your side.'

Collins also booked Louis into a new 'whites only' North Side cellar club called the Showboat. The club was mob-owned and was a place where anything could happen, and usually did. Preston Jackson, who was playing trombone with Louis's band, recalled one night when a gun battle developed and the band had to dive for cover. Drummer Tubby Hall ended up beneath the piano.

Tommy Rockwell did not take kindly to the new situation for he still considered Louis to be contracted to him. Whatever involvement Collins and Rockwell had with the underworld is uncertain, but undoubtedly two gang factions now began to take an undue interest in Louis's career. Louis remembered: 'One night this big, bad-ass hood crashes my dressing room in Chicago and instructs me I will open in such-and-such a club in New York the next night. I tell him I got this Chicago engagement...Then I hear this sound: *snap! click!* I turn around and he has pulled this vast revolver on me and cocked it. *Jesus*, it look like a cannon and sound like death! So I look down at that steel and say. 'Weeelllll, maybe I do open in New York tomorrow.'' Saxophonist George James recalled Mike McKendrick, the band's 'straw-boss', warning the rest of the musicians, 'Pops can get hurt behind this action.' The hood who passed this message to Louis appears to have been a hoodlum named Frankie Foster, but there is confusion as to which New York gang he represented. James Lincoln Collier suggests he

'Looking sharp', in Hollywood 1930.

66

was working for Owney Madden, but if it was Connie's Inn that required Louis's presence, which is most likely, then it is more probable that it was Dutch Schultz's gang or perhaps Mad Dog Coll, who was giving both Schultz and Madden problems during this period.

Rockwell himself made overtures to bring Louis back into the fold and rushed to Chicago to speak with him, but he in turn was threatened in his hotel room, presumably by Johnny Collins's Chicago backers. 'Is this the room Mr Tom Rockwell is in? Well buddy, let me tell you something. The 20th Century leaves town tomorrow morning. You make sure that you get on that train and don't come back to this town again. And stop fooling around with other people's artists.'

For once Louis was spooked. Collins instructed him not to go to New York but to play a theatre date in Chicago, but Louis was adamant, 'I ain't goin' to New York. But get this straight – I ain't staying in Chicago neither . . . I'd rather take a walk through the cemetery at midnight.' Eventually, Collins was able to book Louis and the band on a tour that stretched beyond the 'cotton curtain' with the prestigious stop-over at the Suburban Garden in New Orleans. Once again Louis was to find himself in deep trouble.

Although the New Orleans public, both black and white, was eager to hear 'Little Louie', there was also a racial backlash to greet him. The American Federation of Musicians had banned Louis and the band for not fulfilling the contract with Rockwell, and news of this had filtered through to the local radio station. Preston Jackson recalled, 'They started making announcements over the air about "niggers coming down to New Orleans and taking the white musician's jobs." ' The result of these airings was swift. 'After that we were followed every night . . . by a car with three or four guys in it . . .' The musicians felt intimidated, even those like Jackson who were used to life down South: '. . . it frightened me because my teeth began to chatter, although I was born in that section . . .'

Nevertheless, Louis arrived to a tumultuous welcome. 'When our train pull into the old L & N station out by the Mississippi, at the head of Canal Street, I heard hot music playing. I looked out of the car window and could hardly believe what I saw. There stretched out along the walk were eight bands, all swinging together, wanting to give us a big welcome. As soon as I got off the train the crowd went crazy. They picked me up and put me on their shoulders and started a parade down the centre of Canal Street. Those eight bands almost bust the town open, they made such a noise. Everybody had a good time and

I guess the police did too, because they didn't bother us at all. When they marched around through the city they took me to my hotel for a little rest. My it was a wonderful feeling to go back to your home town and find that while you have been away you have become a big man.' He was also invited back to visit the Waifs' Home. The local press had a field day, reporting on his forthcoming appearance at the Suburban Gardens, which 'was a white man's place. No Negro band had ever played there before. Opening night came and the place was packed.' The performance was to be broadcast. 'All the New Orleans' high society was there. They had a mike in front of the bandstand which was used to broadcast only for white bands.' Although blacks were not allowed into the auditorium they turned up in droves to catch any sound of the performance that might filter outside.

As the audience waited eagerly for the music to commence, the radio announcer broke off his introduction, saying, 'I haven't the heart to announce the nigger on the radio.' Amid the pandemonium which reigned Louis's matter-of-fact acceptance of customs and lifestyle in the South was forcibly demonstrated. Turning to the band, he said, 'Give me a chord', before calmly stepping forward to the microphone to announce himself. 'It was the first time a Negro spoke on the radio down there . . . For the rest of that night and the rest of that gig I did my own radio announcing. That other announcer? They threw him out that same night. Ain't that something?'

A further unsettling incident occurred in New Orleans when an appearance Louis was to make for a black audience was inexplicably cancelled. The crowd was turned away and much of their anger was directed towards Louis.

'One of the most lovable people that ever existed in music . . . Lil was no match for the vultures who surrounded Louis in the most creative days of his career.'

John Hammond

During his engagement at the Suburban Gardens Louis's marriage finally broke down. Lil was phlegmatic: 'You don't need me now you're earning a thousand dollars a week. We'll call it a day.'

Lil had been a tremendous influence upon Louis's career but their personal differences were irreconcilable. They were always to remain friendly and Lil never lost her feeling for Louis.

After they parted she formed several bands herself. Two were 'all-women' units, one of which was called the Harlem Harlicans, with a personnel that included the fine trumpet player Dolly Jones along with Fletcher Henderson's wife, Leona, on trombone, and Hazel Scott's mother, Alma Long Scott, on reeds.

In the mid-1930s Lil fronted a band that had originally belonged to hot violinist Stuff Smith. The band had walked out on Smith after a disagreement and chose a leader from their own ranks. Someone suggested that Lil Armstrong should be asked to front the band, but as George Clark, tenor saxophone with the group, explained, they were not sure that they wanted to be led by a woman. But 'We all fell in love with Lil and we were very sorry that we had selected our own leader because we liked Lil so much.' Although Lil had never completed her time at Fisk University, she had continued her studies elsewhere and gained her Teacher's Diploma in 1928 and a Post-Graduate Diploma in 1929. Dick Vance, another band member, remembered, 'It's been a long time and I've played in a lot of bands but I still think of it as one of the best groups I ever played with.' Trumpet star Jonah Jones agreed. 'It was a great band.' Unfortunately they never recorded and the band suffered from uncaring management. Controlled by the same agency as Louis, the office concentrated on Louis to the detriment of Lil's band. Jonah Jones commented: 'The management just didn't try hard enough...The men in the band would have even worked cheaper just to stay together if it meant more work...We thought that playing good would make us get somewhere. But I found out later that it's the people behind you...I've never had a band play as good as Lil's did...'

In 1936 Lil became house pianist for Decca Records and, as such, made many records with bands and as accompanist to blues singers.

Many of the tunes and arrangements that Louis's Hot Five recorded were by Lil, and she composed such songs as *Brown Gal* and *Old Man Mose*. Her most popular composition was probably *Just for the Thrill*.

George Clark said of her, 'She didn't dwell on any setback or adversity. She just went from one thing to another immediately and with new vigour and new vim and great enthusiasm.' Jonah Jones thought 'this was a most wonderful woman'.

Shortly after Louis's death in 1971, Lil Armstrong died while playing piano at a Louis Armstrong Memorial Concert.

After their stay at the Suburban Gardens in New Orleans
the band played in Houston, Texas, and a number of one-night
stands in the South. Their trail eventually led them to Memphis.

Johnny Collins's wife was responsible for transport
arrangements, and she had chartered a swish Greyhound
vehicle instead of the usual broken-down band bus. When the
band arrived in Memphis the white pedestrians could not
believe their eyes as smartly dressed blacks swept by in a
supercoach, particularly as one, Mike McKendrick, was sitting
up front with a white woman (Mrs Collins), 'just like he was
human'. Louis and the band ended up in jail. Collins was
eventually able to obtain their release, and the band performed
that night at a Memphis hotel. The concert was broadcast, and
his fans back in Harlem were delighted when over the airwaves
they heard Louis dedicate a number to the Memphis Police
Chief: *I'll Be Glad When You're Dead, You Rascal You.*

In their biography of Louis, Max Jones and John Chilton pose
the question: Why, when he was such a success, did Louis
endure the indignities of touring the southern states rather than
perform in the entertainment centres of New York and Chicago?
The answer is that both Collins and Louis were still anxious
to distance themselves from the mob. Back in New York, Connie
Immerman (of Connie's Inn) and Tommy Rockwell failed in
their efforts to bring Louis to court for not fulfilling his contract,
but nevertheless Louis was to feel the brunt of their bitterness.
Eventually, in 1932, he ventured back to New York, but apart
from his making two movie shorts and playing some one-
nighters, few jobs were available to him and his band broke
up. Louis left New York for a brief stay in Los Angeles, then
took up an offer from George Black in London to visit the United
Kingdom for his first tour abroad.

Whether the British public was ready for him or not was
immaterial. Louis still wanted to make himself scarce.

CHAPTER 6

I HATE TO LEAVE YOU NOW

'Jazz is not likely to be continued by decent people.'

Sir Dyce Duckworth

As is common with other nations, jazz has never found great favour with the majority of the British public. On those occasions when it was fashionable, as during the Swing Era and at the time of the Trad Boom of the 1950s, it was always the bland or the novelty aspects of the music that gained most popularity. Much more in common with the comic opera and Music Hall instincts of British theatregoers in the 1920s were the 'black-faced' coon songs of Eugene Stratton and the effete melodies of Layton and Johnson.

The Jubilee Singers of Fisk University introduced the Negro Spiritual to London in 1873 and Queen Victoria was said to have been enchanted by their performance. Although the spiritual continued to be popular with a section of the public, it was the 'Nigger Minstrel' show that took precedence in popular taste. Fondness for the 'blacked-up' minstrel can be traced back to the mid-nineteenth century. Major Dumbeldon's Ethiopian Serenaders toured to some acclaim in 1848, and minstrel shows, including the famous Christy Minstrels, continued to appear in Britain, where they gained great favour in the music halls.

Lacking a local black community in those days, the British public developed a view of the black race almost entirely dependent upon the caricatures of happy but ignorant 'coons' portrayed by the minstrels. Coon acts appeared for many years on Variety bills and G. H. Elliot was still performing as the 'Chocolate Coloured Coon' well into the 1950s. In the 1960s the British public still overwhelmingly accepted the 'Black and White Minstrel Show' on television (the word 'Nigger' being discreetly omitted in deference to the 'enlightened' times).

Genuine black performers appeared regularly in Britain around the beginning of the twentieth century and were accepted as an extension of black-faced minstrelsy with the same condescending goodwill. In 1903 the great American vaudevilleans Bert Williams and George Walker introduced British audiences to the Cakewalk in the all-black show *In Dahomey*. The show offered Londoners a slice of real Negro humour. On other occasions black performers were obliged to adopt minstrel-style billing. When Abbie Mitchell and Her Coloured Students appeared at the Palace Theatre, London, in 1906 their leading performer, Ida Forsyne, was billed as 'Topsy the Famous Negro Dancer'. The *Daily Telegraph* commented: 'If Topsy is not soon the talk of the town we are very much mistaken.' Forsyne did in fact retain her popularity both in England and Europe but kept her demeaning stage name only until her return to America.

In 1912 the Original American Ragtime Octet arrived in London in the middle of a craze for ragtime and made a significant impression upon audiences at the London Hippodrome, where they appeared in *Hello Ragtime*. Ersatz ragtime abounded and songs such as *Ragtime Cowboy Joe* and Irving Berlin's *Alexander's Ragtime Band* proved very popular. The *Musical Mail* commented: 'Like the influenza this "frying pan" music has enveloped us.'

In 1914 the drumming sensation of the day was Louis Mitchell. He arrived in London direct from Harlem and was hailed by London newspapers as 'the World's greatest trap drummer'. He returned to America at the outset of World War I, but in 1915 was back in London playing at Ciro's Supper Club with his Seven Spades. They delighted society audiences and the press called him 'the genius of agility and noise' and 'noise artist supreme'. His syncopated music caught the mood of the day. 'There was no good improvisers in those days,' musician Leo Vauchant commented; 'it started with that orchestra, the Mitchell one.'

When, in 1917, America entered the war, the American 'doughboys' brought with them even more exponents of black music. Large syncopated military bands performed in France and Belgium. General John Pershing, commander of the American Expeditionary Forces, entertained British and French officers at his headquarters with performances by the band of the 369th Infantry Regiment, or 'Hellfighters' as they became known. The Hellfighters band was led by Lieutenant James Reese Europe, a leading pre-war bandleader from Harlem. There were other excellent military bands; one was led by

Lieutenant Will Vodery, another by J. Tim Brymn. Brymn's band was known as the 70 Black Devils of the 350th USA Field Artillery. He described his band's work as a 'Military Symphony Engaged in a Battle of Jazz'.

In his book *The Appeal of Jazz*, published in 1925, R. W. S. Mendl described the musical needs of officers and men on leave from the battle front during the war. 'They needed a powerful stimulant, and the strong rhythms and the bright colours of the syncopated dance orchestra gave it to them.'

As the war ended, Louis Mitchell moved from London to Paris with a new band called the Mitchell's Jazz Kings. As in London, Mitchell soon became the rage, attracting the attention of writer Jean Cocteau: 'There was a barman of noise behind a gilded stand laden with bells, rods, boards and motorcycle horns. He

Mug Shot—1932.

poured these into cocktails putting in a dash of cymbals every now and then, getting up, strutting, and smiling to the angels.'

Mitchell's Jazz Kings included trumpet player Cricket Smith, who had played with Ford Dabney and James R. Europe in New York; and early trombone ace Frank Withers who had originally made his name with the Wilbur Sweatman band. Belgian critic Robert Goffin described the band in his first jazz book, *Aux Frontiers du Jazz*: 'It was the greatest emotion I had ever experienced. A sort of physical shock marked me for life. As far as I can remember, their music consisted mainly of raggy and bumpy ensembles. They left an extraordinary impression.'

The term 'jazz' was in free use in London by 1917 although no one was quite certain whether it was a dance or a form of music. Nick LaRocca's definition did not ease the uncertainty. 'Jazz is the assassination, the murdering, the slaying of syncopation.'

LaRocca's band, The Original Dixieland Jazz Band from New Orleans, appeared in Albert de Courville's West End revue *Joy Belles* at the London Hippodrome. They were not an immediate success; indeed they had little chance to be so. At the insistence of an outraged George Robey, 'The Prime Minister of Mirth' who was topping the bill, the management dismissed them after only one performance. The band later obtained a residency at the newly opened Hammersmith Palais de Danse. Although the Dixielanders never gained the praise of the British press, as had Mitchell's syncopators, they did gain the vote of the people who danced to their music and they worked out a successful season at Hammersmith.

Of more consequence were the concert performances given by Will Marion Cook and His Southern Syncopated Orchestra. Not that Cook's band was a jazz band; its performances were more in keeping with the plantation-operetta productions of Negro stage shows and the syncopated symphonic works of Jim Europe and J. Tim Brymn. This was confirmed by one of Cook's musicians, trumpeter Arthur Briggs. 'We didn't play jazz, we played ragtime.' Theirs was a genteel form of syncopation which went down well with the critic of the London *Times*: '. . . the great point in their favour is that at a bound they can bring us back to the darkies' folk song and melodies that will live long after jazz and ragtime numbers have enjoyed their spell of popularity.' Although lost to the *Times* critic, the significance of the inclusion within the band's ranks of clarinetist Sidney Bechet was decisively pinpointed by the famed Swiss symphony orchestra conductor Ernest Ansermet. He wrote of Bechet's performance in glowing terms. 'There is in the Southern

74

LONDON PALLADIUM
ADJOINING OXFORD CIRCUS TUBE STATION

TWICE NIGHTLY AT 6.30 AND 9.0 P.M.	COMMENCING MONDAY, JULY 18TH, 1932	MATINEES AT 2.30 WEDNESDAY & THURSDAY

VAUDEVILLE'S BIGGEST BILL !!!

JACK HYLTON INTRODUCES FOR THE FIRST TIME IN ENGLAND

LOUIS ARMSTRONG

KING OF THE TRUMPET AND CREATOR OF HIS OWN SONG STYLE

WITH HIS NEW RHYTHM BAND
AND "SNAKE-HIPS" DANCERS TAYLOR AND ALLMAN PRESENTED BY JOHNNY COLLINS

HUGH WAKEFIELD

with ZILLAH BATEMAN AND CO.

IN A CONVULSION OF LAUGHTER IN ONE ACT BY J. GORDON BOSTOCK "WEDNESDAY AT THE RITZ"

PATTI MOORE AND LEWIS
RETURN OF THE GREAT COMEDY TAP DANCERS SAMMY

THE WORLD'S GREATEST CLUB JUGGLERS THREE SWIFTS

THE FAMOUS SINGER OF 'LA REVE PASSE' ROBERT CHISHOLM

THE ROYAL HINDUSTANS

"VALENCIA" TRIO

JOE BROWNING FIRST TIME HERE

WIERE BROTHERS

EDWIN STYLES

MAX MILLER

Topping the bill at the London Palladium—1932.

Syncopated Orchesta an extraordinary clarinet virtuoso who is, so it seems, the first of his race to have composed perfectly formed blues on the clarinet...' This was the first opportunity for British audiences to hear a great jazz soloist. Arthur Briggs explained that 'the only improvising that was done was by Sidney Bechet', although it was not always to the bandleader's liking. In an interview published in *Storyville* magazine, flautist Bertin Salnave remembered Bechet on one occasion moving forward and improvising an accompaniment for Cook's wife Abbie Mitchell, who was singing a selection from Puccini's *Madame Butterfly*. The rendition finished to considerable applause and Cook asked, 'But Sidney, why didn't you ask me?' 'If I had warned you,' replied Bechet, 'you would never have allowed it.'

American bands and musicians continued to visit Britain. In 1923 audiences showered praise upon Paul Whiteman and his orchestra when he introduced the dubious delights of his own symphonic syncopations. Paul Specht's band, featuring the hot trumpet of Frank Guarante, was a popular draw at Lyons

Corner House. Closer to the real thing was the unheralded appearance at the Piccadilly Hotel in 1924 of the Mound City Blue Blowers. Theirs may have been a novelty act but their hokum was combined with real jazz spirit.

1925 saw the arrival in London of the Dixie Duo (singer Noble Sissle and pianist Eubie Blake), one of the first Negro acts of their kind not to black-up for white audiences. The duo's frothy ragtime act fitted readily into the coon-shouting slot on many Variety bills. They appeared alongside such eminent Variety acts as droll comedian Gillie Potter and 'The Great Little Comedian' Little Tich.

In 1926 Lew Leslie's American revue *Blackbirds* played at the London Pavilion. A mixture of ragtime songs and plantation sketches, the show featured the legendary black star Florence Mills. As accompanists Leslie brought over the Plantation Orchestra with trumpeters Pike Davis and Johnny Dunn. Again the show was much more in the minstrel tradition and proved successful.

Equally in evidence in Britain as in America, the Depression was a time of great contrasts. While thousands lined up in dole queues and eked out a meagre existence, society wined and dined in London's West End hotels and restaurants such as the Monseigneur Grill and Ciro's. Society danced to bands that the general public rarely saw, although they could be heard thanks to weekly radio broadcasts. For the musicians who played in these night clubs it was a strange experience. During the day they lived in tough working-class surroundings but each evening played in a luxurious world of opulence and over-indulgence. Inevitably they met the extremes of society. The Prince of Wales was a regular nightclub devotee and, in the course of an evening, musicians could find themselves playing for royalty and even exchanging a few discreet words with them. Afterwards, in one or another of the after-hours gambling clubs, where many musicians would go to relax, they frequently found themselves in conversation with members of London's underworld, some of whom were dance-band enthusiasts. These after-hours gambling clubs flourished in Soho in the late 1920s and early 1930s and catered for bored socialities, musicians, entertainers, and villains. Most of the gangs who frequented the clubs had associations with the Turf, providing protection for race-course bookmakers, claiming prime pitches and collecting debts. Many battles occurred on race-courses such as Epsom and Windsor between rival razor gangs notorious for their violence. One of the most infamous gangs was run by Charles and Henry Sabini. It was rumoured that it was the

Sabinis who roughed up dance-band crooner Al Bowlly's ex-wife when she embarrassed him in an incident at one of London's top clubs. Bowlly was at the time one of the most popular singers in Britain and he found further fame with Ray Noble in America. Despite his popularity, Bowlly had an uneven temperament and was disliked by many who knew him well. He was killed during the London Blitz.

British dance bands in the early 1930s were among the finest in the world. They provided a pleasing repertoire of danceable tunes often mixed with a curious and very English brand of 'silly ass' comedy. The BBC's late night broadcasts, direct from West End night clubs, were among radio's highspots.

But the public did not differentiate between dance music and jazz, and all forms of popular music were classed as belonging to the Jazz Age. The most enlightened band leader performing in Britain during the late 1920s was Manila-born Fred Elizalde. His habit of hiring hot musicians from America proved invaluable to local musicians seeking to assimilate the jazz style. Unfortunately, Elizalde's dedication to jazz proved to be his undoing. After protests from listeners, the BBC stopped broadcasting from the Savoy where he was playing. Elizalde was then ousted from his residency at the hotel, where his modern, jazz orientated, approach was too much for the more conservative patrons.

Appearances in Britain in 1930 by American trumpeters Bunny Berigan and Muggsy Spanier, also saxophonist Jimmy Dorsey, passed unnoticed except by fellow musicians who were duly impressed. A leader in British jazz circles in the early 1930s was composer and arranger Spike Hughes. While most British bandleaders were seeking to dilute the emotion and vitality of jazz, Hughes, in the wake of Elizalde, was composing music of remarkable beauty that, at the same time, gave musicians a solid base upon which they could improvise. A firm favourite with jazz enthusiasts, Hughes never gained nor sought general approval.

Among the leading bands during the 1930s were the show bands of Jack Hylton and Jack Payne and the dance bands of Roy Fox, Harry Roy, Lew Stone, and Ambrose.

Variety theatres were still very popular, and show bands sometimes shared the bill with such entertainers as comedians Will Hay, Max Miller and George Formby. It was only through these appearances that the general public were able to see these London-based bands.

It was in 1932 that Louis Armstrong suddenly burst into this world of music hall comedians, coon acts, jugglers and mild

Louis in London, with pianist Justo Barretto—1933.

dance bands. No one was quite sure how the British public would react. Even those in the know were caught totally unaware by the dramatic stage presence of the great trumpeter.

Louis's imminent arrival caused a stir with Britain's leading music newspaper. *Melody Maker* (which was, according to American jazz critic Dan Morgenstern, 'light years ahead' of similar American publications) commented: 'It is extremely interesting to speculate on what sort of reception Louis

Armstrong will receive from the general public. There is not the slightest doubt of course that he will receive a tumultuous reception from every musician in town...But what of the public? We feel that they, once recovered from the stupefaction, will take Louis to their hearts.'

It was felt that the London Palladium management was being extremely daring in booking Louis, who was virtually unknown to all but a small, if enthusiastic, jazz fraternity. Nevertheless, the *Melody Maker* was of the opinion all would be well: 'The Palladium is sure to be besieged by dance musicians during the engagement. At a conservative estimate 5,000 London readers of *Melody Maker* alone will pay at least one visit...it is a safe bet that the great BP (British Public) will find a thrill in the showmanship and exotic musicianship of the great Negro individualist.'

Louis and his entourage were met at Paddington station by Dan Ingram of *Melody Maker*. Finding that they had no accommodation, Ingram rang a number of hotels and encountered some racial discrimination but was eventually able to obtain hotel rooms. Local trumpet star and Armstrong disciple Nat Gonella happened to be in Boosey & Hawkes' music store and heard that Louis had left his trumpet for repair. Gonella 'begged to be allowed to deliver it to his hotel, refused to hand it over to anyone but Louis and spent a half-hour talking to him in his room. This was undoubtedly one of the great moments of my life.'

Although the house was full each evening at the Palladium it became noticeable that the seats were rapidly vacated before Louis ended his act. Max Jones went to a matinee performance and did not see any such walk-out, but the afternoon performances were usually made up of fans and working musicians who were most enthusiastic. Jones admitted to a certain disquiet at seeing Louis for the first time. 'I was uneasy about someone I thought was great.' It was Louis's overpowering stage presence that alarmed Jones. 'Louis's wild mugging, and his striding around the stage [was] quite different from what we expected.' Jones recalled Louis playing 'a great many high notes and glisses...A far cry from *Mahogany Hall Stomp.'*

If Jones, a self-confessed Armstrong devoteee, was bemused, Louis's detractors had a field day. 'Against all definitions of good taste ... a disgusting exhibition, sure to nauseate all decent men ...' was one example. Even *Melody Maker* commented that the show was 'not suitable for the general public, more for the intimate atmosphere of the nightclub'.

Journalist Hannan Swaffer wrote, 'He resembles a gorged python.' Disdainfully, bandleader Geraldo dismissed Louis as 'a purely freak musician who occupies an illogical position'. Pianist and bandleader Carroll Gibbons came to Louis's defence: 'A gigantic player and supreme originator of style.'

Louis was totally unlike the old-style black performers who had previously appeared in British Variety. Trumpet player Leslie Thompson recalled how he 'would rush on stage and bow his head with growls of "Yah, Yah." ' Introducing *Tiger Rag*, he would flap his arms in the manner of a penguin crying, 'That tiger's travelling fast, gonna take a few choruses to catch him – lookout.' This would be followed by a breakneck version of the tune completed by a series of high notes that would leave the musicians in the audience gasping.

Robert Goffin made a special journey to London to see Louis. His first book had just been published and he had dedicated it to Louis. They met at Victoria Station where Louis was awaiting the arrival by the boat train of the black, mostly American, musicians who were to accompany him. Goffin was to witness the first rehearsal of the band, and described the occasion: 'It was unbelievable. He shut his eyes, flourished his trumpet, twisted his handkerchief, sang in tears, climbed up to hit notes with his neck and cheek so distended that I thought they would burst. What a revelation it was.'

After the first evening's performance Goffin joined Louis in his dressing room where he found ex-boxer Jack Johnson, Nat Gonella, and some other British musicians, along with Johnny Collins and Louis's current girl friend, Alpha Smith. Together they went along to the Monseigneur Grill where Gonella was playing with the Lew Stone band. While they were there Collins involved the group in a drunken scene. Goffin recalled that 'Collins ordered thirty glasses of ale and proceeded to get drunk . . . Collins spoke to me, "Can you fight?" "Yes," I said. "Then I won't pay," Collins shouted . . . We had to carry Collins off like a sack of potatoes and Armstrong signed for the check.'

Although Louis's two weeks at the Palladium were not an unqualified success, neither were they disastrous, and Collins was able to obtain a few bookings in the provinces where Louis was accompanied by British musicians. Apart from the occasional protest, his appearances in Variety and at dance halls were successful. His provincial audiences appeared more willing to accept the Armstrong persona than had their West End counterparts.

It was during his first British tour that Louis gained the nickname which was to stay with him for the rest of his life.

During his early years he had collected many additional names: Little Louie, Dipper, Dippermouth, Pops and Satchelmouth. Louis recalled that it was Percy Mathison Brooks, then editor of *Melody Maker*, who abbreviated the term Satchelmouth to Satchmo, although others have questioned this. Louis remembered Brooks welcoming him and crying out, 'Hello Satchmo!' Later, he asked one of the musicians why Brooks had called him Satchmo. The musician replied, 'It's because you got mo' mouth.' Whether or not it was Brooks, as Louis always claimed, the name stuck and it was as Satchmo that he became known throughout the world.

After his first British tour Louis rested briefly in France nursing a sore lip, then sailed for America and more problems. His arrival in New York coincided with Franklin D. Roosevelt's election as President.

Roosevelt set about the task of allaying the fears of the nation, replacing them with a new optimism based firmly upon positive foundations. In his first hundred days in office he formulated a series of major reforms that were to radically change the face of America. As President he inaugurated a programme of government intervention in industry and business intended to overcome the Great Depression. This included public works on a vast scale, farm subsidies and legislation to liberalize and control relations between the warring factions of capital and labour. The majority of Americans gradually began to feel that perhaps here at last was someone who could solve the country's ills. The repeal of the prohibition laws speedily followed Roosevelt's election.

By 1932 Prohibition had become firmly associated with the Depression in the minds of the general public, and the riddance of one was seen as a sign for the early demise of the other. As folksy philosopher Will Rogers remarked, 'What does prohibition amount to, if your neighbour's children are not eating? It's food, not drink is our problem now. We were so afraid the poor people might drink, now we fixed it so they can't eat . . . The working classes didn't bring this on, it was the big boys that thought the financial drunk was going to last forever.' Viscountess Astor, referring to repeal, commented that the United States was wet when called dry; she suggested hopefully that it would perhaps be dry when it was called wet. She was to be sadly disappointed, for repeal solved nothing. Not only was the Depression to linger, but so too did the mobsters. As the Depression continued it produced a new threat to law and order.

Another kind of criminal, quite unlike the organized city

gangster, began to appear during this period. The crime syndicate, now in the hands of shrewd operators like Lucky Luciano and Bugsy Siegel, continued to thrive, but in the poverty belt in the wastelands of the Mid-West crudely organized gangs carved out short and bloody careers: Ma Barker, Bonnie and Clyde, Machine Gun Kelly, Baby Face Nelson, Pretty Boy Floyd and the most notorious Public Enemy of all, John Dillinger. They robbed stores and banks and, like the gun slingers of the old West, indiscriminately gunned people down. In turn, the miscreants got their just deserts from the hands of J. Edgar Hoover's G-Men.

It was also a time for political opportunists. In Louisiana, Senator Huey P. Long preached 'Robin Hood' style economics while in reality he soaked the poor and bribed the rich. The 'Kingfish', as Long became known, enjoyed his maverick success only briefly and he was shot and killed in 1935, a victim of his own deceits.

'His trumpeting was glorious, his singing delightful; but his band seldom achieved even mediocrity.'

George T. Simon

Louis quickly went back to work after his return to New York, appearing with the Chick Webb band in *Connie's Hot Chocolates* at Harlem's Lafayette Theatre. Then Johnny Collins asked Zilner Randolph to organize another band and they embarked upon a heavy tour schedule.

As Mezz Mezzrow graphically described in his autobiography, Louis was suffering badly with an infected lip. 'He had a terrible sore lip in addition to being dog tired, and that day he had played five shows and made two broadcasts . . . I didn't see how poor old Pops was going to blow note one.' Louis had suffered with lip problems for a number of years. Trumpeter Doc Cheatham considered that it started way back in Chicago when Louis was playing at the Vendome Theatre. 'He used a special Rudy Muck mouthpiece, so sharp it was like a razor on your lip, that's when his lip trouble began.' Earl Hines told Stanley Dance, 'Maybe next day he'd have a little scab on his lip and if he were picking at it I'd ask him, "How're your chops?" "Well, they're *rare!*" he'd say grinning.'

Due to his continuing disagreement with Tommy Rockwell, Louis stopped recording for OKeh and signed with Victor Records although OKeh and its parent company, Columbia, continued to claim him as one of their contracted artists. His first recording session for Victor was made in a converted church. On arriving at the studio, Louis said to Mezz Mezzrow, 'This is funny ain't it Mezza, jammin' in a ole church?' Mezzrow replied, 'Where else should Gabriel blow?' Louis's lip continued to plague him. Mezzrow wrote a vivid account of a performance in Baltimore when Louis's lip was 'so bad, all raw and swole up, that he just sat and looked at it all day in a mirror . . . To make things worse, he kept picking at the great sore with a needle. I couldn't stand to see it . . . "Oh, that's all right Mezz, I been doin' this for a long time . . . got to get them little pieces of dead skin out 'cause they plug up my mouthpiece." His lip looked like he had a big overgrown strawberry setting on it.'

Mezzrow described how chorus girls and performers gathered at the side of the stage that night to see Louis perform. 'He started to blow his chorus, tearing his heart out, and the tones that came vibrating out of those poor agonized lips of his sounded like a weary soul plodding down the lonesome road . . . There was tears in all the eyes around me, tears for what Louis was preaching on that horn, tears for wonderful, overworked, sick and suffering Louis himself, the hero of his race. Everybody knew that each time that horn touched his lips, it was like a red hot poker to him . . . This time for sure he would fail, and break, and collapse with the strain. We heard the torture vibrating behind each searing note. The whole theatre was petrified. Suddenly Charlie "Big" Green busted out in tears and ran off the stand in the middle of a chorus. I saw that the whole band was crying . . . Louis began that tortuous climb up to high F, the notes all agonized and strangled, each one dripping blood . . . Louis clutched and crawled and made that high F on his hands and knees, just barely made it, at the last nerve-slashing second. The whole house . . . rocked with applause. Louis stood there holding his horn and panting, his mangled lip oozing blood.'

Louis's lip problem became common knowledge and gory tales were told resulting in one British press report of his death. A *Daily Express* story in 1933 read, ' "Man With Iron Lips" Killed By His Art . . . died suddenly in a nursing home in New York, a victim to the terrific strain which his art put on him.'

Somehow, Louis was able to continue touring with the band that Zilner Randolph had gathered together. Sideman Scoville Brown recalled how happy he was to be with Louis. 'I couldn't believe it, I was ecstatic, and I went around telling everybody, "I'm going with Louie." ' At first the band was a happy group but gradually, as the hard touring took its toll and Collins paid out meagre wages, their initial enthusiasm dissipated into sullen disenchantment. Nevertheless, their esteem for Louis continued unabated, as Scoville Brown confirmed. 'I can't think of anybody who could thrill you with his horn like he could . . . He'd pick out the seediest girl in the place and come up and give her a kiss on the cheek. He was a nice man. He tried to make everybody feel good. I always remember the time when we repeated some of the places where we had been before. He could call, "Hello Joe", "Hello Amos", "Hello Percival", and he hadn't seen any of these people for a year or so.'

One afternoon in Philadelphia Louis again had problems with mobsters. Two men appeared in his dressing room and Louis, realizing they were after the evening's takings, managed to convey this fact to his valet, who was shrewd enough to remove the money. Immediately his evening performance was over, Louis left the theatre and reported the incident to the local police station. Not unreasonably, he felt that another trip abroad was called for and Collins, who was still having problems with the musicians, was only too happy to disband and arrange another trip to Britain.

Louis's relationship with Collins was at a particularly low ebb. John Hammond, a young member of New York's smart set and a jazz devotee who discovered Billie Holiday, Count Basie and others, recalls one unpleasant confrontation. 'With Louis was his manager Johnny Collins, a man I disliked. One night he got drunk in Louis's stateroom while I upbraided him for using the word "nigger" and for his shabby treatment of Armstrong, who was, after all, Collins's bread and butter. The manager became so furious he took a swing at me. Somehow, for I am certainly no fighter, I managed to counter his punch and knock him on his behind. I think Louis never forgot that fight. It was probably the first time a white man had thought enough of him to fight someone who abused him.'

Returning to Britain, Louis finally parted company with Johnny Collins. Willing to accept the rotten tours, the harsh words, the awful arguments, and even Collins's drunkeness, Louis became aware on his arrival that Collins had not paid taxes due from his last visit. Additionally, payments to his estranged wife, Lil Armstrong, had not been paid. Louis bawled Collins out and Collins left for New York taking with him Louis's passport. The British entrepreneur and bandleader Jack Hylton stepped in and tried to put a little order into Louis's work schedule. He booked him on an extensive tour of the country's Variety theatres and also included a few dance dates.

Louis's first appearance was at London's Holborn Empire,

but critical comment suggested that he should temper his showmanship for the tour. However, when he toured the provinces he encountered very little unfavourable reaction and generally played to ecstatic acclaim. Typical was the Hull *Daily Mail's* review of Louis's performance at the Tivoli Theatre, Hull: ' "I have been among trumpeters all my life, but I never dreamt of the likes o' that." This glowing tribute, from a veteran bandsman ... speaks volumes for the artistry of Louis Armstrong, the world's greatest trumpeter. And it was only one of many similar tributes. Louis's marvellous act brought down the house, and people who had never seen him before shouted his name again and again as he took countless curtains. Seldom has the Tivoli known such enthusiasm. The greatest minutes of all, of course, were when inimitable top notes passed from Armstrong's trumpet bell. Those lips of iron, yet supple as rubber, produced streams of wonderful high notes which no other trumpeter dare even think of playing. Top E natural was played on numerous occasions – almost without an effort. Louis has support from a competent combination of "hot rhythm boys". They play well together and the result, with Louis singing as only he can, and playing in the one and only Armstrong fashion, provides Hull's greatest musical treat for years. Armstrong's noted showmanship is all there and, as usual, he uses countless handkerchiefs ... a wonder trumpet.'

Coleman Hawkins, taking afternoon tea.

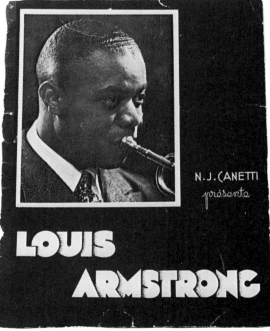

N.J. CANETTI
présente

LOUIS
ARMSTRONG

A Studio portrait in France.

Interestingly, an audience walk-out staged by a classical music appreciation society occurred during his week at the Tivoli. Although the numbers involved are uncertain they were enough for Louis to notice and make a comment from the stage. His words were immediately met by a storm of applause from the rest of the audience, and at the end of the performance he again took endless curtain calls.

While in Hull, Louis also played at a late evening dance. The review of that event reads: 'Lovers of "hot" rhythm had their fill at the Beverley Road Baths, Hull, last night when over 300 people danced to Louis Armstrong's famous Harlem Band . . . considerable interest was aroused in the appearance of such a famous combination on a Hull dance platform. Armstrong's wizardry with his trumpet delighted everyone, and the dance was a decidedly successful innovation.'

Although critics still gibed at his showmanship, Louis's second tour of Britain was a great success. He was also booked by Hylton to tour Denmark, Sweden, Norway and Holland, and while in Denmark made an appearance in a film entitled *Kopenhagen Kalundberg* which featured him in a typical stage performance of the period.

Louis's stay in Britain soured slightly when he backed out of a projected concert appearance at the London Palladium with tenor saxophone star Coleman Hawkins. It is uncertain why he failed to fulfil the booking, particularly as the *Melody Maker* had heavily promoted the show. James Lincoln Collier suggests that Louis had cold feet at the competition from Hawkins, but this can hardly be accepted seriously. Far more likely is the suggestion of 'behind the scenes' management disputes. Nat Gonella commented, 'It had something to do with the money.' Certainly Louis's departure from London forever severed his connection with Jack Hylton. Louis was later to comment, 'When I left London . . . I needed a rest.'

After a brief vacation in Paris, Louis began accepting bookings through the agent N. J. Canetti. His appearance at the Salle Pleyel was one that he always remembered. 'I had to take so many bows until I wound up taking 'em in my bath robe.' By now Louis, aware that his music was something more than simply entertainment, was publicly honoured and feted. He was advertised as the Messiah of Jazz, the Superhuman of the Trumpet, the Real King of Jazz. 'I'd done 13 command performances. I couldn't speak the language, but I always say a note's a note in any language if you hit it on the nose.' Not only was he acclaimed by audiences, he was constantly cornered by earnest critics who would discuss in depth his recorded solos and jazz in general. As Louis remembered, 'That had never happened to me before in America.'

Unfortunately, Louis again had management problems. Canetti booked him on a rigorous tour through Europe even though Louis's lip was in terrible shape as Arthur Briggs testified: '. . . his lips were as hard as a piece of wood and he was bleeding . . . we thought he had some very sad disease.' Briggs described how pus would ooze from Louis's swollen lip. Continually in pain. Louis refused to take part in the tour and was threatened with legal action by Canetti. Wisely, he decided to return to America and in January 1935 he and Alpha Smith sailed back to New York.

CHAPTER 7

SWING THAT MUSIC

'A new era started where Louis the Fighter now became Louis the Champion. Before his career was a matter of seeking and finding. Now he knows. He is above the struggle.'

Hugues Panassié

On returning to America, Louis retreated to Chicago. He didn't blow his horn for six months. Not only was his lip in a terrible state, he was also in an extremely depressed condition due to the interminable management wrangles that beset him. 'Couldn't go no further with all them shysters yiping at me. Everything was in hock. Had a $3200 Buick which was a bitch way back then. Sold it for $390. I decided Joe Glaser was going to be my manager; I had always admired the way he treated his help.'

In Joe Glaser, Louis found a manager who suited him – someone who, for better or worse, would take the responsibilities of bookings, tours, sidemen and all the money matters off his shoulders once and for all. Budd Johnson said of Louis, '. . . he was a guy who always said he didn't want any responsibility at all . . . no hiring no firing. So they took all that away from Louis and just let him play his horn.'

Louis had told Johnson, 'I think I'm goin' to get with old Joe Glaser because he ain't got nothin' and I can tell him what I want.' Glaser, a loud, profane man, was not everyone's idea of an ideal manager. According to Johnson, he had just been released from prison and had links with Chicago gangsters. Reputedly, he ran a prostitution racket on the side and he was not beyond threatening to break the legs of those who displeased him. He did, however, have a quality that inspired trust in those who worked closely with him. Leonard Feather once commented: 'Meeting the irascible Glaser for the first time was an experience some found terrifying. His barking voice was

The irascible Joe Glaser.

tough, his manner abrupt; his language could turn telephones blue. Yet in moments of repose he could be as amiable as a clergyman and as generous as Santa Claus. His integrity was legendary; time and again one would hear the cliché repeated: "Joe Glaser never went back on his word." '

Louis and Glaser had known each other in Chicago during the 1920s at the Sunset Cafe where Glaser's mother owned the building that housed the night club. When they met again in 1935 both men were down on their luck. Louis was unable to play because of his lip and consequently was making no money. Lil was threatening to sue for arrears in maintenance and Alpha Smith was insisting that she and Louis should be married. Johnny Collins was continuing to frustrate Louis's future work plans. To make matters worse, the state of California had notified the narcotics authorities that he had violated his parole by leaving the country. Within a brief time Glaser, to his credit, was able to resolve most of these problems plus the outstanding differences with Tommy Rockwell. In time, Glaser became the most powerful booking agent dealing with jazz and black entertainment in America.

On his return to work after a six-month layoff, there was a noticeable change in Louis's playing. His brilliant supercharged virtuosity, last heard in Europe, had matured into a simplified, more declamatory style while still retaining the same glorious feeling. This new economic, almost austere, delivery allowed Louis to swing even more than before. His 1936 recorded version of *Mahogany Hall Stomp*, although lacking the spontaneity of the original version of 1929, actually swings even more. Now every note is meant to count.

Back in harness and free from the many problems that had frustrated him for so long, Louis took to the road with another band formed by Zilner Randolph. After a brief but strenuous tour, the band broke up and Glaser arranged for Louis to front the Luis Russell band. This association with Russell was to continue for almost a decade.

A gruelling schedule of one-night stands was organized and Glaser was also able to arrange a sponsored radio show. This was a major innovation, the first time a black performer had been sponsored in this way. In 1936 Louis played a role in the Crosby-Astaire film *Pennies from Heaven* and he continued to appear in films for many years. Such relatively unimportant cameo appearances as those in *Every Day's a Holiday, Artists and Models* and the all-black film *Cabin In the Sky* proved to be all-important to Louis's career. They kept him before the general public in America and Europe throughout the Swing

Era when he was performing mainly for black audiences or travelling on obscure Southern circuits.

For Armstrong, the white-dominated Swing Era could have been a disaster. As George T. Simon has written, 'Armstrong was far apart from, and far above the big band with which he worked and it is to his everlasting credit that he not only survived but that he also continued to blow his magnificent horn throughout those years with much feeling and warmth and vitality.'

By 1935 the Swing Era was just getting into its stride. On 21 August of that year Benny Goodman and his band had a great success at the Palomar Ballroom in Los Angeles. George T. Simon had already cited the Goodman band in the March edition of *Metronome* as 'a truly great outfit', and within three years Goodman, by then a national hero, was presented at Carnegie Hall.

Tommy Dorsey formed his own band in 1935 after walking out on his brother Jimmy and their Dorsey Brothers band. To many people Dorsey still epitomizes the Swing Era and the phenomenal upsurge of the white swing bands during the 1930s. Glenn Miller, who found lasting fame a few years later, was still paying his dues in the Ray Noble band in 1935 and Artie Shaw was only just beginning to form a band of his own.

Despite the fame gained by the white big bands, the true innovators were still the black musicians, and top leaders like Goodman, Barnet, Dorsey and Shaw featured black soloists through the era: Cootie Williams, Hot Lips Page, Roy Eldridge, Peanuts Holland, etc. During the 1930s and early 1940s the sounds of swing became a national obsession.

One white trumpet star of the Swing Era was Bunny Berigan. Berigan's surging, all-powerful style was undoubtedly indebted to Louis, and his admiration was reciprocated. Albert Nicholas recalled how Armstrong loved the Berigan horn. When they heard him on the radio, Armstrong would say, 'That's my boy'.

For its playing during its time with Louis, the Russell band has often been condemned by jazz critics and classed as incompetent. Louis's playing during this period has also come under attack. Although in some instances there may be a case to answer, in the majority of recordings Armstrong and the Russell band made together (for Decca), Armstrong was superb and the band gave many excellent contributions. Yet, due to the violent critical reaction, the Russell recordings have been sadly neglected by many jazz enthusiasts and are only rarely re-issued.

Albert Nicholas, who played clarinet with the band, felt that

Louis with the Luis Russell band—1936/7.

90

these were his happiest times: 'We had a hell of a fine band . . . Louis really put the band way out front . . .' Louis himself said, 'The warmth, the feeling . . . everything was there. They were all down to earth also in that band. I love them, regardless what the critics said about us.'

Touring, however, was not easy, as Louis recalled. 'We used to tour the South in a big Packard. Lot of times we wouldn't get a place to sleep. So we'd cross the tracks, pull over to the side of the road and spend the night there. We couldn't get into hotels. Our money wasn't even good. We'd play night clubs and spots which didn't even have a little boys' room for Negroes. When we'd get hungry, my manager, Joe Glaser, who's also my friend, Jewish and white, would buy food along the way in paper bags and bring it to us boys in the bus who couldn't be served . . .'

In 1939 Louis made an interesting departure from his normal schedule to appear at the Center Theatre in New York in the musical play *Swing That Dream*, a black version of Shakespeare's *A Midsummer Night's Dream*. Louis played the part of Bottom but, unfortunately, the play folded after only a brief run.

By the mid-1930s many young trumpet players who had gained their first inspiration from Louis were carving out successful careers for themselves. Among the finest were Cootie Williams, Jonah Jones, Buck Clayton, Bill Coleman, Harry Edison, Joe Thomas, Taft Jordan, Billy Butterfield, Bernie Privin and Bunny Berigan. In reality the list is endless, as every jazz trumpet player was touched in some way by Louis's sound, tone and innovatory greatness. As James Lincoln Collier observes, 'Armstrong had no peer at exposing melody: not Berigan, not [Harry] James or other trumpeters who outstripped him technically, not the virtuoso instrumentalists like Benny Goodman, Tommy Dorsey, Johnny Hodges, who were masters of stating melody. If there were any virtue in a tune Armstrong would find it.'

Henry 'Red' Allen was a major jazz innovator whose own highly original style was initially inspired by Louis and by King Oliver. Allen had the distinction of being the only trumpet soloist to be featured and individually billed in the Russell band during the time when Louis was fronting the group. He was a highly emotional player, full of natural exuberance, and although his style owed a lot to Louis he was too much of an individualist to simply copy him. Red developed a peculiarly rhythmic flexibility, using long melodic lines with unexpected intervals, and in many ways can be said to have extended the Armstrong style. His improvisations were incredibly daring for the time, and it must be said that Allen deserves full credit for his contribution to the development of jazz trumpet in the early 1930s.

Another trumpet player whose style was heavily Armstrong-inspired was Oran 'Hot Lips' Page, who hailed from Texas. Although Lips was unable to match Louis in technique or

King of the Trumpet.

THE KING is COMING

Byron "Speed" Reilly
Takes Pleasure in Presenting—

THE GREATEST OF
★ ATTRACTIONS ★

LOUIE
ARMSTRONG

WITH HIS ORIGINAL
FAMOUS ORCHESTRA

MON. DEC. 20

Sweet's Ballroom

Franklin at 14th St., Oakland, Calif.

ADM. $1.00   DANCE 'till 2

DOORS OPEN — 8:30 p.m.

In Person

The Trumpet
The Personality
The King Himself
With Songs and Hot Tunes

Louie Armstrong

DOORS OPEN — 8:30 p.m.

Oh Boy!—What a night
An A Galaxy of Stars

★ Maestro LUIS RUSSELL
AT THE PIANO

★ Miss Bobbie Caston
HOW THIS BABY SINGS

★ Henry "Red" Allen
"SATCHMO'S" UNDERSTUDY

★ Sonny Woods
YOU'LL LIKE HIS SONGS

18   ARTISTS IN ALL   18
SEE and HEAR THEM with

Louie Armstrong
"KING of the TRUMPET"

AT

SWEET'S

Monday   Dec. 20

imagination, the vehemence of his attack and his powerful tone were enough to bring him to the forefront of horn men in the 1930s and 1940s. Lips captured the essence of Louis's music without ever copying him. His forte was the blues and Dizzy Gillespie once said of him, 'When Lips gets on the blues, don't mess with him; not me, not Roy, not Louis – nobody!'

Charlie Shavers, another brilliant and effervescent trumpet star, was too often dismissed by critics for occasional lapses in taste. Yet his dynamic style was strongly individualistic. His sense of humour was always evident in his playing and he was admired for his brilliant tone, dazzling technique, tremendous power and accuracy.

After Louis, the trumpet player who made the biggest impression in the 1930s was Roy 'Little Jazz' Eldridge. Roy's emotion-filled virtuosity, allied with his vigorous and agile technique, made him the natural successor to Louis in extending the development of jazz trumpet. His more complex approach owed as much to Jabbo Smith as to Louis and yet there is no doubting where his full-bodied, warm tone is derived. His sizzling, agile playing was to alter the direction of an entire generation of musicians. Held in great esteem by his contemporaries, Roy unfortunately never gained great fame, but he was a major influence on jazz trumpet. An extrovert, Roy was more prone than most to taking chances on his horn, and occasionally his solos could lapse into incoherence. Trumpet player Frank Galbreath said of Roy, 'One night I got cut by Roy . . . I didn't feel bad about it because at that time "Little Jazz" could cut just anyone except Satch – and nobody ever cut Louis Armstrong!'

'I used to run up to the Cotton Club . . . every night after work just to hear Pops play a new variation on the Sammy Cahn-Saul Chaplin tune, You're a Lucky Guy. *He never failed me. Every time there was something new.'*

Jimmy Maxwell

It has never been satisfactorily explained why it took Louis so long to play the Cotton Club. Some have suggested that it was because of his disagreement with Tommy Rockwell, while Jim Haskins suggests that Louis was 'a little too Negro' in both his colour and his performance. (The Cotton Club preferred to employ Negroes with light complexions.) Another possibility was Louis's past associations with Connie's Inn, a venue that

Sharing a memory of New Orleans. Henry 'Red' Allen, Louis and Zutty Singleton.

was backed by an opposing gang faction.

Whatever the reasons, they were no longer valid in 1939 when Louis shared top billing at the club first with dancer Bill 'Bojangles' Robinson and later with comedian Stepin Fetchit.

By 1939 the Cotton Club had moved to the top floor of a building on Broadway and 48th Street. The show had none of the usual lavish sets for which the club was famous but it still proved successful. Commenting on Louis's performance, one columnist wrote, 'his trumpet tooting is phenomenal.'

During his stay at the Cotton Club Louis met Lucille Wilson. Although now married to Alpha, Louis was immediately attracted to the chorus girl. He told Luis Russell, 'I like that little chick, put a good word in for me.' Lucille was thrilled but told Russell, 'Just say you haven't had the chance to say anything to me.' Later Louis took her aside. 'See here little girl, I know all the cats are sharking after you; I just want you to know I'm in the running too.'

Louis's relationship with Alpha had never been one of any depth. When she finally left him to run off with a white musician, Louis laconically remarked, 'He's a good drummer.'

Louis married Lucille in 1942 and their marriage lasted until his death. Lucille gave Louis a home and a stability that his life had always lacked. It was a good marriage, although

94

trumpet player Frank Galbreath observed an early side effect. 'When I joined the band Louis . . . was sort of fat, jolly and awfully strong. Oh God, that man had such power and could he blow!! He must have weighed about 220lbs and could he break up a joint! Louis met that cute little chick, Lucille . . . So all of a sudden, Pops decided to make himself slender . . . He started on a diet in 1941 and by 1943 he was down to 135lbs. Man, he was cute, but do you know what? Pops lost so much power. He never realized the reason was this self-imposed diet.' Galbreath described how, on one occasion at the Orpheum Theatre in Los Angeles, Louis was so weak 'someone struck on the idea that Satch would stand in the spotlight with the horn to his lips and I'd stand in the back and do the blowing. And that's what we did! Imagine this!' On another occasion Galbreath took Louis's solo on the first take at a recording session but at the record company's insistence they had to re-record with Louis playing. 'Louis got straight after this had happened and some time later he could blow with his former power again.'

Like every other musician who ever worked with Louis, Galbreath considered him 'a warm hearted and unselfish man'. On one occasion when the band was on air Louis gave Galbreath a long solo on *King Porter Stomp*. The following day Galbreath was really burned up when a newspaper report commented that Louis had played particularly well on that number. 'But Pops was very kind. When he had read the write-up he said. "Smoothie, (his nickname for me) you see, you won't ever get any place here. So if one of those white bands sends for you, make it." In those years a lot of "Spade-cats", especially trumpet players, were joining ofay bands as solo attractions and so, one night in 1943, Charlie Barnet, in New York, needed a trumpet player. I went down and sat in . . . That's how I became a member of the Charlie Barnet band. When I saw Satch again he said to me. "See Smoothie, I told you. This way you'll be able to make yourself a name!" '

Although still with Armstrong, Luis Russell was no longer responsible for running the band. Russell explained, 'I simply got tired of the headaches attendant upon steering a big band for someone else.' Others suggested that Glaser wanted someone who would instil more discipline into the band. Joe Garland took over the role in 1943 while Russell concentrated on playing piano. Louis approved of the change: 'Joe Garland was one of the greatest musicians I ever worked with . . . he would immediately hear a single wrong note . . . Made the band sound nice.'

World War II had been raging in Europe since 1939 but when on 7 December 1941 Japan launched an air attack on the United States' Pacific Fleet at Pearl Harbor, America found itself embroiled in the war against the Axis powers. Within five months the Japanese overran Burma, Hong Kong, Malaya, the Dutch East Indies, Thailand and the Philippines. Congress was obliged to vote over $10,000 million for defence.

Along with every other section of society, musicians were called up for active duty, and the quality of big band music began to deteriorate. The jazz world was also torn apart by the advent of be-bop. The advanced experimentation of young musicians like Charlie Parker, Dizzy Gillespie and Thelonious Monk had the effect of splitting jazz in two. On the one hand were those who wholeheartedly welcomed these musical advances, but there were also those who were totally opposed to any changes.

Although Louis's career had lost some impetus by the early 1940s, suggestions that he was no longer appreciated by the jazz public were not entirely correct. In a letter to the American jazz magazine *Solid State* in 1945, one young enthusiast (Dorothy Gilbert) wrote, 'Before last night we were convinced that Louis was the greatest trumpeter but now we *know* it . . . The band was commercial . . . but never Armstrong . . . You didn't catch a hackneyed phrase in his playing . . . that horn sang out as fresh and original as it ever did twenty years ago . . . The critics always tell how everybody has copied from Louis, but when you hear him he sounds like nobody else.'

In 1942 a dispute between the American Federation of Musicians and the recording companies took musicians out of the studios for almost two years. When Louis Armstrong was able to begin recording again there was a discernible difference in his playing. As the eminent jazz critic Dan Morgenstern observed, 'Modernity is not always a chronological matter. In some ways, Louis Armstrong's most modern playing was done in the mid-40s . . . It is mainly a question of phrasing and harmonic thinking . . . (It is understood that "Modern" is not here meant to indicate superior, as it is in the vocabulary of some jazz writers. In terms of Louis's playing, it simply means that what was in the air in 1945 also fell on his ears—but then, he had a great deal to do with its origins).'

The seeds of modern jazz trumpet were evident in the recorded work of Roy Eldridge and Harry 'Sweets' Edison in the late 1930s. Their solo constructions took a wider, more complex form than those of most other swing trumpeters. They pointed the way to the innovations of the young trumpet men

Louis, 'Hams it up', in
the Hollywood film,
'Going Places'—1938.

who were to be associated with the beginnings of modern jazz
(or, as it was then known, be-bop). Such players included Fats
Navarro, Dizzy Gillespie, Bennie Harris and Howard McGhee.

Dan Morgenstern, one of the few critics to draw attention
to a shift in emphasis that became evident in Louis's phrasing
during the 1940s, explained how his use of longer lines and
descending phrases gave a modern feel to some of his recorded
work, as did his increased use of chord changes. Morgenstern
cites the recording of *You Rascal You* with the Louis Jordan
Jump Band: 'Louis's closing choruses are pitted against a
boppish riff by the band (Wild Bill Davis on piano; Chris
Columbus on drums), and Louis answers with some heavy stuff
of his own. To call it bop would be going too far, but it is a
marvellous example of Louis's ability to respond to fresh and
unusual surroundings.' Other recordings that hint at modernity

are *Jodie Man, Long Long Journey, Snafu, Jack Armstrong Blues* and *Before Long*. Had Louis carried on in this vein who can tell what would have developed, but circumstances were to radically affect his career and his fortunes.

Louis and his band at Loew State Theatre, New York, 1941.

CHAPTER 8

THE REAL AMBASSADOR

'This is one of the greatest musical aggregations of all time – led by America's most gifted creative musician – Louis Armstrong.'
                                                        Fred Robbins

Louis Armstrong's concert at New York's Town Hall on 24 August 1947 irrevocably put an end to his big-band career. Joe Glaser had been against the idea of an Armstrong small group although a number of people had suggested such a switch. Ernest Anderson, who promoted the concert, had great difficulty in convincing Glaser that it was good strategy. In a filmed interview he recalled, 'I'd been trying to get Glaser to put Louis in with a small group . . . You see he was playing one-nighters then for as little as $350 to $650 – with a 16-piece band. They paid the $650 for Saturday nights. And through 1945-6 . . . he did nothing but those one-night stands . . . I went to the bank . . . and had a draft made out to Glaser for $1000. I . . . got the switchboard girl to go in and hand him the cheque. Next thing, the door opened and Joe was demanding, "What's this?" . . . I said that to explain it I'd have to come in. He said he'd give me five minutes. Well, I talked about the 350 for Louis and the whole band and the thousand bucks, and told him I had a date at the Town Hall for a Saturday night. "Give me Louis for a thousand . . . and leave the 16 men behind." . . . if you put a thousand dollars in Glaser's hand, you'd never get that back. So I got Louis for a thousand . . . and then fixed up Tea for $75 the night. Hackett got 50. The rest you know: Peanuts Hucko, Wettling and Catlett for drummers, Bob Haggart and Dick Carey . . . All the musicians were thrilled about it, you know, and everybody was cold sober when it started. It went great. The hall sold out on the night, no question about that, and all kinds of press and musicians were present. The music was marvellous and so were the notices. Glaser was there, of course, and he was thrilled . . . So Louis finished his dates and never went out with a big band again.'

The press, suddenly aware once more of Louis Armstrong, was ecstatic in its acclamation of his genius and his importance. Wilder Hobson wrote that it was 'superb hot music, showing this art form at its best'. Ira Levin, in *downbeat*, stated that 'at all times it was trumpet playing with grace, sincerity, and emotion-packed tone'. In Europe, Carlos De Radzitzky, commenting on the euphoric reviews, noted that 'at last it seems that America recognizes him to be the greatest jazz musician.'

The Town Hall concert, although a turning point in Louis's career, was not his first return to a small group format. In the late 1930s a movement to re-introduce the 'old time' jazz began to develop in America. Forgotten heroes like Sidney Bechet, Muggsy Spanier and Bunk Johnson re-appeared on the jazz scene to renew their recording careers. Decca Records produced jazz collections associated with the 1920s. An album featuring white musicians identified with 'Chicago Style' included groups led by Eddie Condon, Jimmy McPartland and George Wettling. Another collection featured the music of Kansas City and included Pete Johnson, Hot Lips Page, Count Basie and blues shouter Joe Turner. An album of New Orleans music featuring specially created groups led by Red Allen, Zutty Singleton, Johnny Dodds and Jimmie Noone included four sides by Louis and his old colleague Sidney Bechet, who remarked: 'The time I remember that [could] have come closest to playing with someone where I didn't have all the worrying business, someone where I could just relax and go with the music, that was with Louis Armstrong for some recordings we made in 1940.'

Louis, Billie Holiday and Barney Bigard in a publicity still for the film, 'New Orleans'.

The All Stars are launched in Los Angeles—1947. Earl Hines, Jack Teagarden, Louis, Cozy Cole, Barney Bigard and Arvell Shaw.

Unfortunately, Bechet's hopes were not fully realized and there were suggestions that this studio session was marred by a clash of temperaments. Bechet himself said, 'I felt sad at the way these records went with Louis . . . Louis knew it too.' Lil Armstrong, who was working for Decca, did the arranging, and according to Bechet, 'she came to me and she told me, "Sidney, go ahead just like you want. Play the way you want, like we've been wanting to hear you. You're with Louis. You'll both be together and you'll both be really able to play." Because she knew how Louis and I can do it.' When they began to record, however, Bechet felt that 'it seemed like [Louis] was wanting to make it a kind of thing where we were supposed to be bucking each other'. Claude Jones, who played trombone on the session, viewed it differently. 'Louis and Bechet were in peak form that day but the recording manager just wore me down. He kept coming out of his sound-proof box, and shouting, "Give that horn more tailgate Jones, more tailgate," and he got me so mad in the end I messed up my solo on *Down in Honky Tonk Town*.' Whatever the truth, the tracks made at that session, although less than perfect, certainly had many inspired moments. Vic Bellerby, reviewing a reissue of these recordings, observed that 'music like this is rare and wonderful'. In 1945 Bechet and Armstrong again joined forces and played together at an *Esquire* concert held in New Orleans. Bechet said later, 'I had a lot of pleasure playing with Louis again.'

101

Louis had taken leave of his big band on another occasion in 1944 when he took part in the First Esquire All Star Concert which presented top musicians chosen by *Esquire* magazine. The concert, which took place at the Metropolitan Opera House in New York, was emceed by critic Leonard Feather and featured a truly all-star lineup: Roy Eldridge, Jack Teagarden, Barney Bigard, Coleman Hawkins, Art Tatum, Al Casey, Oscar Pettiford, Sid Catlett, Billie Holiday, Red Norvo and Lionel Hampton. The concert was organized at short notice and the musicians had little time to rehearse. Consequently, although many splendid solos were heard, a lack of group cohesion was evident. The concert, however, was favourably reviewed and *Esquire* was encouraged to finance a similar event a year later.

Another small-group session of considerable importance that involved Louis occurred in 1944 as part of the US Government's V Disc programme. Issued during the war years for the 'recreation of American GIs', V Discs, which supposedly remained the property of the United States Government, were first produced in 1942 and were mostly pressed at the Victor and Columbia factories. All major American recording artists were featured on V Disc and the American Federation of Musicians allowed its members to record free of charge as a contribution to the war effort. This was done on the understanding that all masters would be destroyed when peace was restored. Fortunately for the sake of succeeding generations of fans, a mild touch of larceny occurred and many V Discs survived.

One such survivor was a three-hour session in 1944 to which Louis, then appearing at the Club Zanzibar, was invited. In the company of musicians such as Jack Teagarden, Bobby Hackett and Billy Butterfield, Louis played magnificently.

1946 proved an eventful year for Louis: he recorded with the Esquire Award All Stars, who included Charlie Shavers, Johnny Hodges and Duke Ellington. In the same year he went to Hollywood to appear in the film *New Orleans*. While he was there a record session was organized by Leonard Feather and a set of recordings was released to coincide with the film. In the film, Louis's band consisted of Barney Bigard, Kid Ory, Charlie Beal, Red Callender, Bud Scott and Zutty Singleton. Feather wanted a more modern line-up and so substituted trombonist Vic Dickenson and guitarist Allan Reuss for Ory and Scott.

Feather later recalled visiting Louis on the set at Hal Roach Studios, where he found the band listening to recordings of primitive New Orleans music provided by the studio. Expected

A 1947 Esquire All Star concert bill.

to listen to and learn from them, instead 'they erupted in roars of laughter at the welter of wrong notes, out-of-tune horns, and generally unspeakable non-music.'

Later in 1946, Feather presented Louis at a concert at Carnegie Hall with the Ed Hall Sextet. Glaser, who wanted Louis to use a big band, persuaded Feather to share the programme: one half to the Sextet, the other to the big band.

The film *New Orleans* went on general release in 1947 and was given a showbiz premiere in New York. A concert arranged for opening night was broadcast by NBC from the Winter Garden Theatre. The band's personnel was similar to that for the Town Hall concert a month earlier.

'Way back, I set myself to be a happy man, and made it.'

Louis Armstrong

In 1947 Louis, now in his late forties, entered the most hectic phase of his already busy career. Yet, although his fame grew to phenomenal proportions and brought him enormous financial gain, it all meant little to him. When not travelling (which he did for most of each year) he continued to live in relatively modest surroundings at the home that Lucille had made for him in the Corona Section of Queens, New York.

The All Stars' debut as a working unit occurred at Billy Berg's Club in Los Angeles. Among the celebrities who attended were Johnny Mercer, Bing Crosby, Hoagy Carmichael, Benny Goodman and Woody Herman. The press gave the new group considerable coverage as it was considered an important move, a return to Louis's jazz roots.

More than ever before, Louis found himself in the limelight. The All Stars were big news. Earl Hines had joined Jack Teagarden, Sid Catlett and, along with Barney Bigard on clarinet, they were in every sense a really all-star line-up. Jazz critic George Avakian described the band as a group which 'does not pretend to be a Dixieland band, nor does it offer anything new or sensational in music. Satchmo's superb stage presence binds together a showcase of jazz stars into a stage production that warmed the hearts of nostalgic music lovers . . . Louis is playing and singing with more heart and inspiration than he has for years.'

The format that Louis used proved to be totally successful and has since been adopted by traditional and mainstream

Between sets.
Big Sid Catlett, Louis,
Barney Bigard and
Earl Hines.

groups the world over. Many bands blithely consider themselves either to be New Orleans or Dixieland bands, when in fact what they are using is the all-star format that links a string of solo performances within loose arrangements. This requires a degree of skill and imagination if the listener's interest is to be sustained, and only the finest jazz musicians are able to do this satisfactorily. Few bands using the all-star formula manage to retain the spirit or the swing of the Armstrong All Stars.

In 1948 the first All Stars were invited to the Nice Jazz Festival in France. It was Louis's first visit to Europe since 1934 and was considered very important by his management. The war which had devastated Europe was over, more than a dozen years had elapsed since European audiences had seen Louis in person and his stature in the rapidly changing jazz scene was in question. Understandably, everyone was uncertain what European response would be but, equally, all were sure that success here would be an invaluable boost to his career.

On the flight over from America Louis took part in a radio interview, and listeners were able to hear Louis, Teagarden and Bigard jamming on board the aircraft.

The furore caused by his appearance in Nice was amazing. Humphrey Lyttelton, who was himself appearing at the festival, described how Louis had only to emerge from his hotel for the street to be blocked by thousands of fans clamouring for autographs. Musicians would cram into Louis's dressing room to hear the great man warming up. Commenting on Louis's playing, Lyttelton said, 'I was particularly struck by the almost puritanical simplicity of his playing ... with its purity and serenity.'

Although Louis left all business responsibilities to others, on stage there was only one man in charge. In his autobiography, Lyttelton describes how he stood behind the bandstand one night while the All Stars played and on more than one occasion found himself 'quaking at the ferocity with which he directed the band. If Sid Catlett's drums started to intrude too heavily upon a solo, Louis would turn and hiss at him like a snake. And more than once Earl Hines's exuberance was curbed by a sharp, "Cut it, Boy!" '

Recalling the Nice Festival, Earl Hines said, 'When we travelled to Europe I was a little upset that he had so little time for us. I naturally remembered the years when we used to run around and hang out together. But later I found it wasn't *his* fault. He was a giant of jazz ... and did wonderful things in Europe.'

Arvell Shaw, bass player with the All Stars for many years, had no doubts that Louis's authority was necessary. 'The All Stars were a very special kind of group but without Armstrong it wouldn't have been anything. His personality was so strong he could carry any group right along with him. He was a very smart man and realized that even with his talent he needed the very best musicians which is what he had: Jack Teagarden, Earl Hines, Sid Catlett, Barney Bigard, Trummy Young, Ed Hall, Cozy Cole, Billy Kyle, Barrett Deems and, thank goodness, I was able to be part of it.'

The All Star years can be loosely split into three periods. The first was between 1947 and 1954 with a band of truly star soloists like Teagarden, Hines, Catlett, Cole and Bigard. The second between 1954 and 1956 featured sidemen like Billy Kyle, Trummy Young and Ed Hall. In the final period from 1956 on, there were frequent changes in the personnel. Some sidemen proved to be good while others were indifferent.

Gradually the band's concert repertoire became subject to severe criticism for being repetitive, and many leading critics stopped listening to Louis in the late 1950s and in consequence missed a further decade of wonderful music. American critics were by far the most guilty of such oversights. Contradicting the prevailing opinion, Canadian critic John Norris wrote to *Jazz Journal* in 1957 saying, 'I went to hear Louis at the Basin Street Club ... New York. Having been to most of his London concerts ... I wanted to find out whether the damaging statements [made] by leading US critics were true. Was it possible that Louis had played differently in England than on

Louis, enjoying the applause.

his home territory, or was it just a major divergence in tastes and opinions? . . . To my ears there was little, if any, difference in the standard of performance of the band or in the presentation of the numbers. The attack and drive of Louis's trumpet playing was just as wonderful, with the rich full tone that no one else can match. Both leading and behind other soloists, his playing was a joy to listen to . . .' Norris went on to ask, 'Why then is it that critics in the US and England have such differing views on Louis Armstrong? Can it be that there is a completely different concept as to what is of value in jazz music?'

David Halberstam concurred with this 'minority' view. 'I had gone . . . to write a twilight-of-career piece about him. It's perfectly true that he paces himself carefully but the essence of the trumpet is all there, still able to touch a man in almost any mood; and the voice, deep and gravelly, is still expressive, light and flirtatious or deep and sentimental.'

Off-stage, too, there was dissent, but this was of a much more fundamental nature, raising as it did the recurring conflict between blacks and whites in America.

In the years following World War II American Negroes had become less prepared to accept the degrading everyday conditions of their lives in a white-dominated society. They had fought and been prepared to die for their country. The least they expected in return was equality. It was easier hoped for than achieved. Pre-war black entertainers were caught in the backlash of opinion and were greatly criticized by militant blacks who considered their stage presentation subservient and

Smile for the camera. All Stars, Cozy Cole, Jack Teagarden, Louis, Arvell Shaw, Barney Bigard, Earl Hines.

degrading. In America, Louis became saddled with this 'Uncle Tom' image.

Dizzy Gillespie, a young musician who was by then a leader among modern jazz trumpet players, later commented on Louis: '. . . if anybody asked me about a certain public image of him, handkerchief on his head, grinning in the face of white racism, I never hesitated to say I didn't like it . . . Later on, I began to recognise [it] as his refusal to let anything, even anger about racism, steal the joy from his life.'

Not everybody was as far-sighted as Gillespie. Writer David Houlden pointed out the disparity of some critical reporting that was typical of the times. 'Armstrong's foolin' is reported as, "Uncle Tom", but Gillespie's clowning is referred to as possessing "a Chaplinesque sense of the ridiculous". Again it was said that Ed Hall (then an Armstrong sideman) is "being turned into a third rate comedian", but Dizzy's tenorman, doing shuffle on a comedy number was reported as [having] "a sense of timing worthy of a Stan Laurel." '

Two American critics at the Newport Festival in 1957 felt obliged to instruct Louis on how to change his stage performance and received a salty reply. 'Write anything you want to write but don't tell me how to play my horn.' Louis told Sinclair Traill that many people asked why the band did not play more new tunes. His response illuminated his approach to his work: 'Well y'know it's a real consolation always gettin' that note – just hittin' it right. The public can get to know you better by them old tunes than by anything new. So, like Heifetz and Marian Anderson, we play the same tunes: every time they play the same solo they get applause – so do we.' Importantly there was more for Louis than mere consolation – he was enjoying himself. 'It don't really make no difference where I blow my horn as long as the guys behind me are playing right. But still and all I prefer the small band. I've had some good big bands, they were well rehearsed. But a leader's got to be able to instil himself into a band. Where there's too many men it's hard to get that feeling like Joe Oliver and I had, like Jack Teagarden and I have.'

Louis was becoming increasingly known and loved by thousands upon thousands of fans both old and new, many of whom were only vaguely aware of jazz. But, while continuing to play set routines in concert halls around the globe, he did manage to produce record albums that were in many ways the equal of anything he had ever recorded.

During the 1950s, discrimination in the record industry relaxed to a very great extent. Black artists were promoted as

never before. Mixed jazz groups became an everyday occurrence. It was a far cry from the 1930s when Louis was one of the select few black performers to appear with white musicians and when someone as respected as Benny Goodman was forced to reject the inclusion of Coleman Hawkins at a record date. 'If it gets around that I record with coloured guys I won't get another job in this town,' Goodman had declared.

This change of circumstances was more a result of commercial alertness than of any deep social consciousness. Independent record companies catering exclusively to black audiences for black music worked on a regional basis with limited circulation. In the post-war years a number of distributors realized the immense commercial potential in black music and especially the most popular form: Rhythm and Blues. They began to organize national distribution networks, and this led to a rise in importance of a new breed of popular black artists and brought an influx of rhythmic excitement to the bland white popular music scene. This tremendous success led people to forget the groundwork done in very different circumstances by an earlier generation of black artists which included Louis, Duke Ellington, Ethel Waters, Lena Horne and Fats Waller.

Breaking 'em up.
Louis and Velma Middleton doing their routine.

Still friends.
Lil and Louis have fun in Paris in the 1950s.

108

Newport Blues.
Jack Teagarden and
Louis.

'*The way they are treating my people in the South, the government can go to hell. President Eisenhower has no guts.*'

Louis Armstrong

During the 1950s, with the southern states of America deep in the throes of resistance to change, discrimination was at a particularly violent stage in the nation's history. While visiting New Orleans in 1949 Louis had been crowned 'King of the Zulus'. The mayor of the city said to him, 'I've always heard it said that you felt you would die happy if you were made the King of the Zulus.' Louis replied, 'That's right, all I hope is that the good Lord don't take me too literally.' By the 1950s his opinion of his home town had changed. He told Max Jones, 'I don't care if I ever see that city again. Honestly, they treat me better all over the world than they do in my home town. Ain't that stupid? Jazz was born there and I remember when it wasn't no crime for cats of *any* colour to get together and blow.'

Louis's unhappiness at racial injustice in America turned to anger and he finally erupted in the American national press after he had watched violent scenes on TV during the school integration furore at Little Rock, Arkansas, in 1957.

For years Louis had been abused by some critics for his 'Uncle Tomming'. Now his forthright condemnation of the government's lack of action in Little Rock and his personal criticism of President Eisenhower brought mixed response. One columnist called him 'an ingrate' while Sammy Davis Jr commented on TV: 'You cannot voice an opinion about a situation which is basically discrimination, integration etc, and then go out and appear before segregated audiences...For years Louis Armstrong has been important in the newspapers. They have always been ready to give space if he had anything to say that really was an important thing, and he never has. Now this happens. I don't think it honest. If it is, why didn't he say it ten years ago? He doesn't need a segregated audience.'

Contrary to Davis's criticism, Louis's statement was as

Louis and Lucille arrive in Sweden.

honest as anything he had ever said in public. After a lifetime when to open his mouth could have meant the end of a job, his career, or even his life, the scenes from Little Rock were so shocking that on the spur of the moment he relaxed his guard and placed himself in the centre of an arena of which he knew little. 'I don't dive into politics, haven't voted since I've lived in New York, ain't no messing with something you don't know anything about.' If Davis could not understand this, at least he could have applauded the truth of Louis's statement. Louis had once remarked: 'You don't pose, never, that's the last thing you do because the minute you pose you're through as a jazzman.' For Louis, a totally non-political person, to issue considered statements as Davis suggested would have been ludicrous. Louis's message was in his music.

He cancelled a proposed tour of the Soviet Union saying, 'The people over there ask me, "What's with my country?" What am I supposed to say?' Still bruised by the incident, Louis made further comments while in Denmark. 'They would beat Jesus if he was black and marched.' Defending Louis's angry outburst, Max Kaminsky said, 'I think it was what Louis said that got Ike [Eisenhower] up off his rear over this Little Rock business. That episode is one hell of a smear over America, and it takes a hell of a lot of guts for Louis to stand up and say the things he said. Louis is not an Uncle Tom. He's a great man, apart from the fact that he's the greatest jazz trumpet player that ever lived.'

If Louis could see no breakthrough in his own country, elsewhere he was more optimisitic. He played in both East and West Germany and when asked what he thought about the nation's re-unification he replied, 'Unify Germany? Why man, we've *already* unified it! We came through Germany blowin' this old happy music and if the Germans ain't unified, this ain't old Satchmo talkin' to ya.' Asked if he would still like to tour Russia, he said 'They ain't so cold but what we couldn't bruise them with the happy music.'

Foreign travel played an increasingly important part in Louis's itinerary and took him to many and varied destinations where the effect he had upon people was amazing. Trumpeter Charlie Shavers suggested a motivation: 'Louis is the kind of person that just can't keep still. He loves the roar of the crowd at the end of shows, so he must keep going or he'll fade away. Louis is such a vital man that he must keep going places and doing things; and you take that away from him and he'll run down like a clock. He's been going too many years now to stop all of a sudden.'

Louis and the All Stars in Ghana.

Peter Black, TV critic for the London *Daily Mail,* wrote, 'When Eurovision brings us something that we want to see it reminds us of how pitifully television, for reasons mainly political, wastes what should be one of its strongest weapons. Louis Armstrong and his band, shown on BBC and Granada from the Italian resort of Viareggio, provided one of those occasions. It did you good just to look at him. I cannot pose as an expert on his subject. I suggest with diffidence that the entertainment was optimistic, encouraging, and quite noticeably stimulating. But this may have been only the emanations from Armstrong's personality. Sweat ran down his face. When he sang you imagined his vocal chords as thick as ropes. When he blew his trumpet you would not have been surprised if the whole man had suddenly gone off bang. He looked the incarnation of the spirit of fun; and he looked 110% alive, a kindly, generous being whom I would unhesitatingly accept as world leader.'

Edward R. Murrow made an hour-long CBS TV programme about Louis which was later expanded into a film entitled *Satchmo the Great* and released in 1957. It covered Louis's hectic lifestyle and in particular the All Stars' tour of Africa. Despite much talk of State Department sponsorship, Louis did in fact get very little help from the government for his world trips which did so much to engender goodwill for his country. Sponsorship for his African tour came mainly from Pepsi-Cola, and, as can be seen in the film, the trip was very successful. Lucille Armstrong commented. 'The treatment we got during the whole tour was wonderful. Everywhere they took to Louis's music and came in thousands.' Lucille and Velma Middleton,

112

the band's singer, were invited to visit a harem, 'a thing which had never been done before'. At this point Louis, who was listening to his wife, chipped in, 'Yeh, but that old Sultan wouldn't let me in, even when I tol' him none of them ladies had anything Lucille hadn't got – but better.'

The value of Louis's overseas tours did not pass unnoticed in America and in 1958, after playing for the House of Representatives of the State of Massachusetts, Louis received a citation from the legislature.

The citation read:

> Whereas Louis Armstrong, the World's greatest trumpeter in the field of jazz music is about to celebrate his fiftieth year as a musician; and
>
> Whereas, Louis Armstrong by his artistry has through the universal language of music brought comfort, pleasure and understanding to people throughout the world, and is properly recognized as the outstanding ambassador of good will of our country, therefore be it Resolved, that the
>
> Massachusetts Senate extends its best wishes to Louis Armstrong and wishes him many years of health and happiness, so that he may continue to spread happiness for all people; and be it further
>
> Resolved that copies of these resolutions be transmitted forthwith by the clerk of the Senate to Louis Armstrong.

Ed Hall and Louis enthuse while Trummy blows.

The touring continued, with Louis commenting: 'These one-nighters aren't so bad. You gotta take care of yourself. I play them because I love music. I can make it in New York without trouble but I don't mind travelling and that's what I want, the audience. I want to hear their applause. Hell, I made money when I was a kid driving a coal cart in New Orleans, and I've got all I need now. But I'm a musician and I still got to blow.'

Then suddenly in 1959, during a long European tour, the 'man of iron' showed the first sign of strain. Booked to appear at a music festival at Spoleto, Italy, Louis collapsed and was taken to hospital. The jazz world held its breath. Louis's physician, Doctor Alexander Schiff, announced his patient had pneumonia but, in fact, he had suffered a severe heart attack. Expecting Louis to be out of action for some time, everyone was startled when he left hospital after only one week and was performing within another five days. Jack Teagarden expressed surprise at seeing Louis, let alone having him join in for a set with the band.

In the 1960s musicians still marvelled at the quality of Louis's playing. In 1967 Rex Stewart told Sinclair Traill, 'Louis can be marvellous! When he's in shape, as he was when he was at Monterey with us, he is wonderful. That night he played as I haven't heard him play in twenty years – he gassed everybody. And the band with Tyree Glenn and Buster Bailey were so right – it is funny it hasn't happened before. Buster is very good for him, for he needs someone to push him, make him extend himself.' Earlier in 1965 Ruby Braff explained to Sinclair Traill how extraordinary he thought Louis was. 'The only one who ever was that kind of a virtuoso, and yet at the same time a fantastic musician. In other words his great virtuosity never interfered at all with his jazz—he had just the perfect combination of everything.' Braff went on to berate those who were no longer listening to Louis. 'I spent three days this year listening to him play at Freedom Lane ____ I hung out and never missed a note. So stupid, none of those smart musicians in New York were there. He played so great, so fantastic – and none of those smart critics, who only live such a short distance away, bothered to come and hear him. What those ____ missed!'

Louis was still touring as strenuously as ever, although his medicine chest was now ever larger. Included in its contents was a massive supply of laxatives, for Louis's reliance on such aids was legendary, and in particular his liking for a brand named 'Swiss Kriss'. Bass player Jack Lesberg described to Sinclair Traill how Louis had persuaded a well-known classical musician and conductor to take some Swiss Kriss. 'There he

The stylish Billy Kyle. When the All Stars were refused accommodation at a Swiss Hotel, Billy was heard to remark, 'This must be the South of Switzerland.'

was, clad in immaculate tails, waving his baton conducting the big orchestra until suddenly he hurled his stick in the air and without a moment's delay disappeared under the orchestra pit to parts unknown.' Louis also persuaded Lesberg to take similar treatment with the same result. 'Well, I woke up in the night and made it along that corridor like an Olympic sprint champion. I really burnt up the carpet. I don't know what happened to that orchestra conductor, but I certainly never made it.'

Also legendary was Louis's all-embracing view of religion and religious leaders. 'I'm a Baptist and *good* friend of the Pope, and I always wear a Jewish Star for luck.' Once, during an audience with the Pope, he was asked by the Pontiff, 'Have you any children?' Louis replied, 'No, but we're still right in their wailin', Daddy!' Jack Lesberg also recalled that when he was planning a holiday in Rome, Louis insisted that he should visit the Pope. ' "Don't worry Pops," Louis said, "I'll write him a note." . . . he wrote, "Dear Pope, This is my friend and bass player Jack Lesberg. He'll be coming to see you . . ." '

Sinclair Traill neatly summed up the Louis legend when he said, 'His famous remarks are legion and have been quoted many times but don't forget they were all true.'

During Lyndon Johnson's term as President of the United States (1963-68) a campaign was mounted by several writers

Vocalist, Jewel Brown watches, while Trummy and Joe Darensburg accompany Louis.

and officials to obtain a special award for Louis. Among the writers involved was Ralph J. Gleason. 'We wrote letters to Congressmen and officials. I even got from the US Information Agency the names of people on the President's Commission who were to make the awards and wrote to each of them.' The result was less than satisfactory. According to Gleason, Texan-born Lyndon Johnson stayed true to the code of the South. He could not bring himself to approve the award.

If Louis was not appreciated by the White House he certainly was by fellow musicians.

Trummy Young: 'I get a spark playing with him that I never had with any other trumpet man. He gets the feeling for his music over, not only to the audience but to his band as well. As for still having it, well, all the other trumpet players are always telling me, "Cut Down Trummy, cut down, go easy" but Louis just says, "Blow Trummy, blow". That guy does it every night and I think he's got a bigger tone, a lot fuller than before. I've picked up timing and pacing by working with him, but what I like best of all is that he's always on top of the trombone, clear and simple, none of this bubbling stuff. There are guys who can blow more notes, but I've never seen anyone who can go on top of him.'

Max Kaminsky: 'With all his genius he has never lost his perspective. Louis knows who he is. Not only that, he knows who you are, and though he is the most approachable, most genuine, person in the world, and though his charity is legendary, you can't mess with Louis. He has kept straight with himself because his trumpet comes first – that's Louis . . . To him his playing is a gift and he'll just sit there and think about his horn before he gets ready to play – accepting his gift he calls it . . . Louis has never forgotten what he wants to do – just play that music – and in doing just that he has done everything.'

Marty Napoleon: 'Whenever I hear his name I remember the great music but most of all I recall a warm generous man with simple tastes who knew how to be happy and how to make others happy. And unlike so many others in the music business, Louis Armstrong wasn't a phoney.'

Gene Krupa: 'I knew immediately when I heard Louis at Chicago's Lincoln Garden in 1922 that he had it all.'

Johnny Hodges: 'Well, after Louis I don't hear no more trumpet players! I can easily forget about all the others . . .'

Wild Bill Davison: 'Just to be able to make one note sound like Louis is enough to accomplish in a lifetime.'

Randy Brecker: 'I suppose in a way Louis Armstrong influenced every trumpet player who has come along since his

Louis and Lucille in the 'den'.

116

time. Those old players played just what they heard – it was like as if they were singing to themselves. I think it's a pity that that philosophy of playing is lacking in the new music. It's very hard to do, but I try to combine the things I work out at home with those things I hear and like. I just sing to myself and then play; which is what Louis Armstrong did, and was really how jazz got started. Vocalization of the jazz instrument.'

As the 1960s drew to a close Louis's health was deteriorating, as was his playing. Eventually he had to put down his horn and concentrate on the other tool of his trade – his singing voice.

Way back in the streets of New Orleans Louis had been singing long before he ever played the cornet. His earliest recorded vocal was with the Fletcher Henderson band in 1925, and reputedly his scatting on the Hot Five recording of *Heebie Jeebies* was the first of its kind to be recorded. Many hundreds of jazz vocalists have followed his lead and used scat singing

Louis mugs while Lionel Hampton and Dizzy Gillespie look on.

118

but few have ever equalled him. As Louis explained, 'What's scattin' but notes – but the right notes. Just to be scattin' and makin' a whole lotta noise and faces slobbin' all over yourself. No. Let them notes come out right . . .' No one could do that better than Louis. James Lincoln Collier wrote, 'You could warm your hands in front of Louis Armstrong. You could not be unhappy when he was singing.'

Louis's vocals proved very popular in the 1960s, and in 1964 he had a big hit with *Hello Dolly*. Arvell Shaw recalled how Louis and the band were called back to the studios to record the number and Louis became irritated after looking at the tune, saying, 'You mean you brought me in on my afternoon off to record this rubbish?' Later during a tour the band began to hear their audiences calling, 'Hello Dolly, Hello Dolly.' Louis asked, 'What is it they're calling?' Billy Kyle reminded him, 'It's that song we recorded.' They had to get the office to send the music so that they could learn it. When eventually they performed it at a concert, 'it brought the house down'.

In 1968 Louis topped hit parades all around the world with a vocal record: *What a Wonderful World*. He was still a winner, someone of whom his race and his country could be justly proud.

Quincy Jones once said, 'You know it's easy to be stingy with your soul, but it takes a real big cat like Louis Armstrong – which is why everybody loves Pops – who can still play jazz and still be commercial. Pops reaches the people but keeps it jazz because he keeps it free. You have to be big to be able to communicate with simplicity. And you know, you can be just as modern being simple as you can being complex.'

In 1971 Louis Armstrong suffered another heart attack and entered Beth Israel Hospital, New York, on 15 March. He was in intensive care for several weeks but at his own request was taken home in early May. On 6 July at 5.30am he died in his sleep.

His fellow jazz giant Duke Ellington, himself very ill, issued a statement: 'If anyone was Mr Jazz, it was Louis Armstrong. He was the epitome of jazz and always will be. Every trumpet player who decided he wanted to lean towards the American idiom was influenced by him. He inspired thousands of people to play the same instrument, and to try to play the Louis Armstrong style. In some cases, their own individuality broke through, and some of his best and most sincere imitators became really great too. He is what I call an American standard, an American original. It is a great loss because he is irreplaceable, and we are going to miss him terribly. I love him. God bless him.'

120

CHAPTER 9

SATCHMOGRAPHY

'. . . his playing and singing, live or recorded, is an inexhaustible source of joy, inspiration and faith. . .'
                                                                          Dan Morgenstern

Compiling a discography for any prolific artist is a specialized and ultimately self-defeating task. New issues and re-issues of the recordings of major jazz artists appear regularly, only to be withdrawn or deleted within a short time. Old albums appear in partially or totally new guises – often with new titles and lacking in details of recording dates and personnel. For these reasons the recordings cited are identified by title wherever possible and by last-known label and number. Many of the records will be available only from specialist jazz record shops and, even then, in the second-hand racks.

Where American labels/numbers are indicated, the tracks included may not always be identical to the British counterpart.

Any reader seeking additional information on recording sessions, including full personnel details, is directed to the comprehensive discography *Boy from New Orleans – Louis Armstrong* by Hans Westerberg published by Jazzmedia ApS, Copenhagen, Denmark.

Over a number of years critics have gone to great lengths to point to the defects within Louis's recorded works while, at times, understating their positive qualities. The sniping at the Hot Five and Seven recordings, the dismissal of his big band output and barely concealed scorn for the All Star sides, has ensured that many of his masterpieces are unknown to all but the keenest of today's jazz fans. From his earliest recordings with King Oliver to the albums made at the very end of his career, Louis was always worthy of attention. Even in the late 1960s his albums still had quality and, at times, a touch of genius.

The musical importance of Louis's Hot Five and Seven recordings can never be overstated, but how much of it would have come about without his experience with the larger bands of Henderson, Tate and Dickerson? His work with these aggregations broadened his concepts far beyond the boundaries of New Orleans collective improvisation and made possible the startling progress evidenced in the Hot Five and Seven sides. By the time he changed from recording with small groups to his own big bands, his imagination and facility had so outstripped his fellow musicians that the much maligned accompanying function adopted by his orchestras was the only sensible approach. Any alternative would have stifled Louis's imaginative outpourings and inevitably limited the effect he had upon generations of great jazz soloists.

Whilst no longer advancing the course of jazz, his All Star years occasionally offered recordings of sheer excellence, the equal of almost everything that had gone before. Newcomers to jazz should search out the following recordings, for they capture the genius of Louis and illustrate, far better than any words, his all-powerful influence which will forever pervade the world of jazz.

Louis's recording career began with King Oliver and his Creole Jazz Band in 1923. His first recorded solo occurs on *Chimes Blues* and he produces 24 bars of confident and well-constructed cornet playing. Eighteen of Oliver's Gennett and Paramount recordings, including *Chimes Bues*, appear on 'Louis Armstrong and King Oliver' (Milestone double album M 47017). During the same year the band also recorded for the OKeh Record Company. Fifteen of these sides make up a splendid album on World Records Retrieval Series SH 358, 'The Okeh Session – King Oliver and his Creole Jazz Band'.

Highly disciplined interpretations are contained on both the Milestone and the World Records albums. Played with a joyous warmth of expression and extraordinary unity, the individual roles of each musician integrate into overall band performances of special beauty. The instrumental textures contained within these logical, even predictable, ensembles give the lie to the supposed incompatibility of band discipline and jazz expression. The OKeh sides are marginally superior both in sound quality and band performance. This is evident on duplicated titles such as *Dippermouth Blues, Snake Rag,* and *Riverside Blues.* The sharper-sounding OKeh sides allow the listener to identify clearly Louis's second cornet part, particularly on the lovely *Mabel's Dream.* All of these performances were acoustically recorded but it is still possible for the listener to absorb some

122

of the excitement that the cornet breaks of Oliver and Louis generated back in Chicago in the early 1920s. It is remarkable that Louis, one of the greatest and most exuberant solo performers of all time, could contain himself so well within the strict confines of such an intricate yet orderly ensemble.

The Milestone album also benefits from the inclusion of seven Gennett recordings by the Red Onion Jazz Babies, a studio group organized by Clarence Williams during Louis's first visit to New York in 1924. They include three tracks that find Louis in the company of Sidney Bechet: *Nobody Knows the Way I Feel This Morning, Early Every Morn, Cakewalking Babies from Home*. Although they are not quite as clean-cut as the Clarence Williams Blue Five recordings made for OKeh during the same period, they do serve to show Louis's progression from second cornet to lead. The quality of the Blue Five is illustrated on Fontana TFL 5087 (in the US, Smithsonian RO26), 'Sidney Bechet Memorial'. Again the better sound of the early OKeh recordings enables the listener to perceive that Louis was the equal of the already mature Bechet. Louis's characteristic descending arpeggios and high-note 'rips' are already discernible as Bechet relentlessly weaves his hypnotic filigrees around the powerful cornet lead. A vivacious *Cakewalking Babies from Home* and vibrant *Texas Moaner Blues* show clearly the rhythmic advancement which these two young innovators had attained by the mid-1920s.

Further proof can be found in the recordings of the Fletcher Henderson band. 'Louis Armstrong with the Fletcher Henderson Orchestra' (VJM VLP60) clearly shows Louis's advanced solos to be embarrassingly superior to those of his fellow section members Howard Scott and Elmer Chambers. The insipid repertoire of the early Henderson band invariably comes alive only when Louis cuts through with his searing hot solos. His startling attack bursts through the undistinguished band sound on *How Come You Do Me Like You Do* and *I'll See You in My Dreams*. *Everybody Loves My Baby* (take 1), features Louis's first recorded vocal. A further two titles appear on Classic Jazz Masters CJM 88507, 'Fletcher Henderson Orchestra with Louis Armstrong and Coleman Hawkins'. Louis transforms two mundane band performances on *Mandy Make Up Your Mind* and *Prince of Wails* with his infectious solos. Unleashed from the collective format to which he was accustomed and no longer required to stay in the middle register, he begins to investigate the wider range of his horn. It was not long before he would fully utilize this new-found freedom.

Louis's skill as an accompanist became evident while he was in New York. He began to record with many of the leading blues singers and cabaret artists of the day. Included on Swaggie S1258, 'Bessie Smith, Vol 1' are the superlative recordings made by Bessie and Louis. No finer classic blues performances exist. The exquisite displays of both singer and musician on *J. C. Holmes Blues, Careless Love Blues, Sobbin' Hearted Blues* and *St Louis Blues* are simply beautiful.

Collectors Classics CC33, 'Louis Armstrong/Blues Singers' includes *Broken Busted Blues, My John Blues* and *Shipwrecked Blues* with Clara Smith and some rarely re-issued sides on which Louis accompanies Chippie Hill, Nolan Welch and Blanche Calloway (these latter sides all being recorded in Chicago).

Obscure recordings by Louis accompanying Ma Rainey; Trixie Smith and the vaudeville team of Coot Grant and Wesley Wilson are gathered together as part of a double album on Kings of Jazz NCJ 18001/2. Included are such rarities as *Find Me at the Greasy Spoon (If You Miss Me Here)* and *Come On Coot Do That Thing* by Grant and Wilson; *The World's Jazz Crazy and So Am I* and *The Railroad Blues* by Trixie Smith, and *Jelly Bean Blues* and *Countin' the Blues* with Ma Rainey. They all feature Louis's soulful and blues-drenched horn.

An unusual collection appears on Swaggie S1310, 'Louis Armstrong, The Blues Singers 1925-1929'. The album features sides made with Hocial Thomas (the earthiest of blues singers), the volatile blues queen Victoria Spivey and Lillian Delk Christian. Miss Christian is totally forgettable but her accompaniment is something else. Louis, along with clarinetist Jimmie Noone and pianist Earl Hines, shares the honours in providing delightful and sensitive backing for the harmless vocals on *Too Busy, I Can't Give You Anything But Love, Sweethearts on Parade* and *Baby.*

MCA 1301, 'Young Louis: the Sideman (1924-27)' gathers together some interesting performances. The earliest item is a rarely re-issued *Words* by the Fletcher Henderson band; also included are two sides by Perry Bradfords's Jazz Phools, *Lucy Long* and *Ain't Gonna Play No Second Fiddle.* These tracks have in the past been damned by faint praise but nevertheless show Louis playing a strong lead and delivering a driving solo on the latter title. Other titles that appear on this album are by Jimmy Bertrand's Washboard Wizards, Johnny Dodds' Black Bottom Stompers and Lil's Hot Shots. They could be described as the alternative Louis, for they were all made for Vocalion while Louis was contracted to OKeh in the mid-1920s. In contrast to his OKeh output during the same period, Louis plays a sober lead which at times appears inhibited. Presumably he was trying to disguise his identity and consequently gives performances much closer to his New Orleans origins. In complete contrast, two very exciting titles are included on this album, *Static Strut* and *Stomp Off, Let's Go*, which Louis made with Erskine Tate's Vendome Orchestra. They are of considerable importance, showing Louis in the context of an excellent big-band performance playing two flashy and exuberant trumpet solos.

The Hot Five and Seven recordings made for OKeh are all included on a 4-album set issued on World Records SM421-4 (in the US, Columbia CL851-4), 'The Louis Armstrong Legend 1925-29'. These are undoubtedly among the finest jazz recordings ever produced, charting as they do Louis's progress from his first realization of his own potential on early titles *My Heart*, *Yes! I'm in the Barrel*, through to the assured and positive brilliance of *Weather Bird*, *West End Blues* and the informal New York recording of *Knockin' a Jug*.

On *Heebie Jeebies* Louis's easy singing captures the imagination. This was an early best seller with its impromptu scat vocal. Louis's exceptional performance on *Oriental Strut* and the stop-time chorus and breaks of *Cornet Chop Suey* give exciting and ample warning of the thrilling recordings that were yet to come. The two-bar breaks of *Skid Dat De Dat* and the imaginative logic of Louis's solo on *Big Butter and Egg Man* pre-empt exciting and remarkable performances like *Potato Head Blues* with its famous stop-time chorus, or the spectacular breaks heard on *The Last Time*.

It must be noted that while the other members of the early Hot Five are not as advanced as Louis, they do acquit themselves admirably, often brilliantly, within their limitations. The fact that they are limited in comparison to Louis does not invalidate their contributions on these sides. At times Johnny Dodds is at his very greatest, and Johnny St Cyr gives a remarkable performance throughout as sole rhythm performer. The brilliant high notes and triplets on *Struttin' with Some Barbecue* show Armstrong at his most vital. The inclusion of guitarist Lonnie Johnson on *I'm Not Rough*, *Hotter Than That* and *Savoy Blues* brings an added authority to these titles and provides Louis with additional incentive to produce solos of ever-increasing stature.

West End Blues recorded in 1928 is still considered to be one of Louis's finest achievements with its famous introductory cadenza and uncluttered yet blistering build-up which climaxes with an impassioned and perfect finale. The band now included Earl Hines and Zutty Singleton and they sparkle on *Skip the Gutter*, *Muggles* and *Beau Koo Jack*. Perhaps the finest of all these sides is the duet performance on *Weather Bird*. Louis and Hines combine to produce a bravura performance second to none. Throughout, they anticipate each other's move as each in turn throws down the gauntlet. It is a performance of spontaneous creativity and extraordinary rapport.

Other tracks on this 4-record set that are of particular interest are *Symphonic Raps*, *Savoyagers Stomp* and *Chicago Breakdown* by Louis and the Carroll Dickerson Orchestra. The first two are by Dickerson's band which played at the Savoy Ballroom and the latter by his band from the Sunset Cafe in Chicago. They show Louis with working bands as opposed to the studio groups with which he normally recorded during the period. Another title included in this set is *Knockin' a Jug*, the first recording Louis made in New York after his return to the city in 1929. On this informal session he is joined for the first time on record by Jack Teagarden and both give imaginative performances.

Extremely fine examples of Louis's early big-band recordings can be found on Swaggie S1402-3 (in the US, DRG Swing 8451), 'Louis Armstrong and his Orchestra 1929-1931'. A perfect tempo and a powerful beat generated by Pops Foster's bass give a stimulating setting for Louis on *Mahogany Hall Stomp*. Louis's superb tone and timing, backed by the full sound of the Luis Russell band, makes this one of the all-time great performances. Charlie Holmes, Lonnie Johnson and J. C. Higginbotham also contribute solos of considerable quality. Other powerful performances with the Russell band are registered on *Dallas Blues* and *I Can't Give You Anything But Love*. There are also good examples of the band which Zilner Randolph formed for Louis and show him in magnificent form. He stamps his authority firmly over less-than-perfect accompaniment, his virtuosity and drive being quite breathtaking. *Wrap Your Troubles in Dreams*, *Between the Devil and the Deep Blue Sea*, *Lazy River* and *Stardust* are supreme interpretations full of spontaneity, warmth and drive.

Swaggie S1265, 'Louis Armstrong—Louis in Los Angeles 1930', brings together all of the titles Louis made with the Sebastian Cotton Club orchestra and is a truly wonderful album. The infectious *I'm a Ding Dong Daddy from Dumas*, with scalding hot trumpet, and a poised *I'm In the Market for You*, with its superlative last chorus, vie for greatness with other amazing performances such as *I'm Confessin'*, *If I Could*

Be with You, Sweethearts on Parade and *Just a Gigolo*. Also included on this album is the definitive version of *Dear Old Southland* with Louis accompanied only by Buck Washington on piano.

Louis's assurance and his obvious delight in his technique are evident in the Victor recordings of 1932-3. They are included on RCA Black & White double album, Jazz Tribune, 'Young Louis Armstrong (1930-1933)', NL89747 (Bluebird AXM2-5519). Louis's beautifully buoyant solo on *That's My Home* (both takes) are among his greatest, and he is backed by a swinging Chick Webb band. Other beautiful solos occur on *I Hate To Leave You Now, Honey Don't You Love Me Anymore, Dusky Stevedore, Mississippi Basin, I've Got the World On a String* and *Basin Street Blues*. These last five titles were recorded with the Zilner Randolph band. Louis's execution is both flexible and assured, his tone pure and his phrasing well defined. All of these recordings require repeated listening in order that every facet of his unique conception can be caught.

Louis made six sides while he was in Europe in 1934 and they all appear on Polydor Select 2344045 (Onyx 213), 'Tootin' Through the Roof: Volume 2'. Made in Paris, they feature Louis's flamboyant trumpet backed by a band that accompanied him in Europe, including the Hines-inspired pianist Herman

Louis takes a bow with the Dandridge Sisters and Bill 'Bojangles' Robinson at the Apollo Theatre—1939.

127

Chittison. *Super Tiger Rag* is an outstanding version featuring a show-stopping performance by Louis of staggering virtuosity. Both takes of *St Louis Blues* are included and Louis uses quite different quotes in each version. *Song of the Vipers* appears to be quite abstract, featuring unusual vocalizing by Louis and more vociferous horn. *Will You, Won't You Be My Baby* and *Sunny Side of the Street (Parts 1 & 2)* are quite excellent with beautifully conceived performances by Louis.

Some of Louis's early recordings for Decca appear on MCA Coral, Jazz Heritage CP1 (in the US, MCA 1312), 'Louis Armstrong and His Orchestra (1935-44) Swing That Music'. Louis is backed by the Luis Russell band. The solid anchor of Pops Foster's bass and Paul Barbarin's drumming again gives Louis a firm foundation. This is notable on *Eventide, Thank's a Million, Jubilee* and *Strutting with Some Barbecue*. With trombonist J.C. Higginbotham and trumpeter Henry 'Red' Allen returning to the band, Louis had soloists who could enliven and enhance the overall band performance and this is very evident on this album. In Shelton Hemphill the band had one of the finest lead trumpets available, and the alto saxophone of Charlie Holmes and clarinet of Albert Nicholas could always be counted upon to supply solos of grace and invention. When drummer Big Sid Catlett replaced Paul Barbarin in 1939 his presence brought a new dimension to the band's performance which can be heard on *You're a Lucky Guy, Everthing's Been Done Before,* and *Hey Lawdy Mama*. Ace of Hearts AH7, 'Louis Armstrong Jazz Classics' also features some excellent tracks by this band: *Mahogany Hall Stomp, Bye and Bye, Wolverine Blues, When the Saints Go Marching In, Savoy Blues* and one isolated example of Louis working with the Jimmy Dorsey Orchestra, *Dippermouth Blues*.

Rarities 50, 'The Rare Louis Armstrong – The Big Band 1943-44', shows the big band during the final years of its existence and includes a number of titles not often associated with Louis: *In the Mood, I Never Knew, King Porter Stomp, Coquette*.

Louis's 1940 recordings with Sidney Bechet appear on Brunswick LAT8146, 'New Orleans Jazz'. Four sides are included and provide some very mellow moments with tight interplay between Louis and Bechet on *Coal Cart Blues,* Sidney's magnificent soprano saxophone on *Down in Honky Tonk Town* and Louis's poignant vocal on *2.19 Blues*. His driving trumpet throughout these remarkable sides certainly brings into question Bechet's less than complimentary remarks regarding the session.

The First Esquire Concert of 1944 has been issued on Saga Pan 6922 and 6923. Although the sound quality is uneven the performances of all the participants make these recordings invaluable, with Louis performing particularly well.

Pumpkin 103, 'Midnight at V-Disc', includes takes 1 and 2 of *Play Me the Blues* and *I'm Confessin'* which show Louis in quite devastating form. His playing is brimful of fire and power with distinctly 'modern' overtones. In contrast, RCA International INTS 5070, 'Town Hall Concert Plus – Louis Armstrong and His Orchestra' portrays Louis in a variety of moods. Six tracks are from the famous New York Town Hall Concert: *Rockin' Chair, Ain't Misbehavin', Back o' Town Blues, Pennies from Heaven, St James Infirmary, Save it Pretty Mama.* They show Louis to be using a more austere, declamatory style which is filled with excitement. *Snafu* and *Long, Long Journey,* recorded with the Esquire Award Winners, show Louis in a rather more modern mood, while *Mahogany Hall Stomp* is more reactionary, with a band similar to that which appeared in the film New Orleans (Minor Hall replacing Zutty Singleton). *I Want a Little Girl* and *Sugar* are by the band that Leonard Feather rearranged and Louis finds the amended personnel quite a stimulant and produces two delightful performances. Later, French RCA issued 'The Complete Town Hall Concert,

1947' which includes tunes previously unissued due to poor quality of sound. (PM 45374)

The soundtrack from the film *New Orleans* is issued on Giants of Jazz Records GOJ-1025-A. Again, the mood is deliberately reactionary, with Louis quite at home in the setting and playing with rare vigour.

Louis's visit to the Nice Jazz Festival in 1948 is well documented on Musidisc Jazz Anthology 30JA5154-5, 'Louis Armstrong—Integral Nice Concert 1948, Volumes 1-2'. Most of the tracks included on these two albums were recorded at the festival and, although the sound quality is poor, the music is totally convincing. Far superior in quality of sound are the concert performances on Brunswick LAT 8017-8, 'Satchmo At Symphony Hall Volumes 1 and 2' (in the US, MCA2 4057). These two albums show the first All Star group at its best. Jack Teagarden is superb on his feature number, *Stars Fell on Alabama*, as is Barney Bigard on *Tea for Two* where he particularly sparkles during a duet with drummer Sid Catlett. Catlett's extended drum feature *Boff Boff* is a show piece of masterly drumming. Throughout the two albums Louis drives along with intense power. *Muskrat Ramble, Black and Blue, Royal Garden Blues*, offer just some of the delights available on this excellent live recording.

'Satchmo at Pasadena' Brunswick LAT 8019 (the US issue on MCA is out of print), another live recording, although not quite as exhilarating as the Symphony Hall concert, has the bonus of featuring the effervescent Earl Hines on piano, and he successfully establishes his personality over every track, particularly *My Monday Date*. An exceptional version of *Indiana* featuring Hines, Bigard, Louis and Teagarden give this album particular impetus. Louis is a powerhouse throughout all of the albums that feature the first All Star group, and although prodigious solos are forthcoming from all those participating, Louis remains majestically in command.

A 2-volume set on Brunswick LAT 8084-5, 'Gene Norman Presents Louis Armstrong At the Crescendo – Volumes 1-2', provides an early example of the second All Star period. Teagarden and Hines are replaced by Trummy Young and Billy Kyle, while the drum chair is taken over by Barrett Deems. Although the album is chock-full of cheerful music and Louis performs magnificently on titles such as *Back o' Town Blues, Tin Roof Blues,* and *Lazy River*, we have to look at their studio performances before we see them at their cohesive best.

The album that is generally cited for showing the All Stars at their best is 'Louis Armstrong Plays W.C. Handy', CBS 21128

130

(in the US, CSP JCL 591). The surviving two members of the group, Barrett Deems and Arvell Shaw, both consider it to be their finest achievement, as they well might, for it captures the group in splendid form. The propulsive trombone playing of Trummy Young complements Louis's mellow horn and the pleasure that both get from each other's playing is evident. Young's roaring uninhibited trombone rips its way through the ensemble, inspiring Louis to soar enthusiastically over the rocking combo, at times leaving a slightly underrecorded Bigard battling to make himself heard. A nine-minute version of *St Louis Blues* is the finest recorded example of the tune since Louis's original version made with Bessie Smith in 1925. Velma Middleton may not be in the same class as Bessie but this remains a superb recording. *Yellow Dog Blues, Loveless Love, Aunt Hager's Blues* swing along in a way that suits Louis and Trummy, and together they raise the roof. On *Atlanta Blues* Louis accompanies his own vocal with enormous effect, and he and Velma both have fun with *Long Gone*. A better balance is evident on *Memphis Blues*, and Bigard comes more into his own, although honours inevitably go to Louis and front line partner Trummy Young. Trummy, as ever, is the perfect foil for Louis, with Billy Kyle's piano complementing them both, especially on *Beale Street Blues*. Louis exposes the melody to telling effect on all of these W.C. Handy blues. Still able to surprise with an unusual turn of phrase, he continues to do just that on *Ole Miss, Chantez-Les-Bas* and *Hesitating Blues*.

Another album of equal quality is 'Satch Plays Fats' on CBS 21103 (in the US, CSP JCL 708), an album made up of tunes composed by Fats Waller. Louis and the band perform with warm sincerity on tunes like *Honeysuckle Rose, Blue Turning Grey Over You* and *I'm Crazy 'Bout My Baby*. Again Louis's singing and playing are immaculate, with Trummy's trombone giving each performance an incredible vigour, and overall this album is marginally superior to the more revered Handy album. The often criticized Barrett Deems succeeds in driving the band along, ably supported by the ever-dependable Arvell Shaw on bass. Immense swing is achieved on every track, especially on *Keepin' Out of Mischief Now, All That Meat and No Potatoes, I've Got a Feeling I'm Falling, Black and Blue* and *Ain't Misbehavin'*, with Louis straddling each performance with infinite ease and majestic style.

With CBS 21121 (in the US, CSP JCL 840), 'Ambassador Satch', the band returns to the concert format and a distinctly different balance is immediately discernible in the ensemble. The difference in sound is attributable to the inclusion of Ed

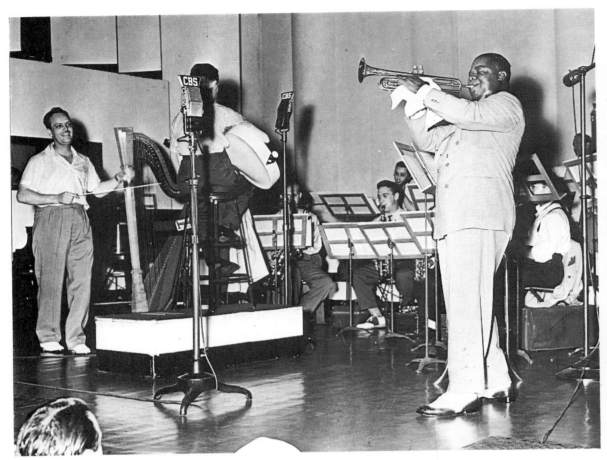

Saturday Night Swing Shift.
Leith Stevens conducts, Louis swings, on a CBS Radio broadcast—1938.

Hall as replacement for Bigard. His thick tone and attacking style are much more suitable for the aggressive All Star style, and his clarinet can be heard cutting through the rugged sounds emanating from the other two front-line horns. There is some doubt exactly where these sides were recorded but it is generally believed that they originated at concerts in Holland and Italy. Wherever it was, the concert hall excitement of a Satchmo performance is effectively captured. *Royal Garden Blues* gives a rousing start to the album, with vigorous solos from Louis, Ed and Trummy. Equally exciting, *The Faithful Hussar* roars to its swinging conclusion after an unscheduled reprise. Louis scats an unexpected chorus to the surprise of the rest of the band and the delight of an enthusiastic audience. *All of Me* and *Muskrat Ramble* are full of interpolated quotes, and again Ed Hall adds immeasurably to the overall balance of the group. The hokum of *Twelfth Street Rag* comes as welcome relief, such is the intensity of the performances. Space is reserved for extended solos by Trummy Young on *Undecided* and Ed Hall

132

on *Dardanella*. Billy Kyle and the rhythm section support the front line ably and Louis's *West End Blues* produces yet another masterpiece. 'Ambassador Satch' is arguably the hottest concert recording Louis ever made.

In 1956 Louis recorded a 4-record set for Brunswick, LAT 8211-4, 'A Musical Autobiography' (in the US, MCA2 4173/4), in which he creates afresh masterworks on tunes with which he was associatied during his younger days. With the exception of a few re-issues all the numbers were specially recorded and show Louis still a master of the jazz idiom. Record 1 contains re-creations of tunes associated with the King Oliver band and the Classic Blues sides that Louis made in the 1920s. On *Dippermouth Blues* Yank Lawson takes King Oliver's place as lead trumpet and Louis plays second until it is time for the famous solo. This time Louis performs it prodigiously. There is some fine clarinet from Ed Hall on *Canal Street Blues,* and throughout Billy Kyle plays extremely well on piano. Velma Middleton sings the blues and, while not the equal of the original singers, she does perform adequately.

Record 2 reproduces the tunes originally recorded by the Hot Five. Trummy Young plays a fine solo on *Georgia Grind,* and some fiery trumpet is heard on *King of the Zulus. Wild Man Blues* is a nicely relaxed performance with powerful trumpet and excellent clarinet. *Weary Blues* and *Hotter Than That* are two swinging tracks on which everyone plays well. Record 3 has some superior trumpet playing by Louis and exemplary piano from Billy Kyle on two tunes associated with Earl Hines, *Two Deuces* and *My Monday Date. Knockin' a Jug* has an augmented All Star group swinging away, with solos by Trummy Young, guitarist Everett Barksdale, and tenor saxophonist Seldon Powell, in addition to Louis. Louis plays some high-register trumpet on *I Can't Give You Anything But Love* while Ed Hall's agile clarinet takes the prize on *Mahogany Hall Stomp.* Louis's solo performance on *Dear Old Southland* is rich and beautiful as is his playing on *Some Of These Days* and *When You're Smiling.*

If I Could Be with You, Body and Soul, Them There Eyes, That's My Home and *Sunny Side of the Street* on Record 4 all offer delightful, and at times brilliant, trumpet from Louis with Ed Hall performing particularly well on *Them There Eyes* and Trummy Young giving Louis fine support on *Lazy River.* This entire set is quite magnificent, and while not innovatory, as were the originals, in many cases Louis's solos are better conceived and better played.

On 'Louis and the Good Book', Brunswick LAT 8270 (in the

US, MCA 1300), Louis plays and sings twelve spirituals. His tone and phrasing aptly demonstrate the affinity between jazz and this kind of material. He gives tasteful performances on *Go Down Moses, Down by the Riverside, Didn't It Rain* and particularly on *Rock My Soul*. The accompaniment is by the All Stars and a choir directed by Sy Oliver.

RCA International INTS 1084 (in the US, Audio Fidelity AFSK-6132), 'The Best of Louis Armstrong', was recorded in 1959 with Peanuts Hucko, Mort Herbert and Danny Barcelona replacing Hall, Shaw and Deems. The choice of material is interesting, *Doctor Jazz, Frankie and Johnny, I Ain't Gonna Give Nobody None of This Jelly Roll, Old Kentucky Home* and *I Ain't Got Nobody* being new to the band. Hucko plays well, as do Trummy Young and Billy Kyle, while Louis's playing is glorious. Other titles of particular interest are *Chimes Blues* and a splendid version of the old Lil's Hot Shots number, *Drop That Sack*. Throughout the album the choice of tempi is impeccable.

In 1960 Louis joined forces briefly with the Dukes of Dixieland and produced an album of surprising quality. 'Yeah', Fontana FJL 116 has Louis in tremendous form. Although the

Big T, Barney and Satch help Mickey Rooney work on his rim shots.
Taken on the set of the 1951 film, 'The Strip'.

accompanying band is stodgy and at times plods dreadfully, Louis sails through some interesting tunes and is obviously buoyed by the change of company. *Bourbon Street Parade, Washington and Lee Swing* and *Just a Closer Walk with Thee* are some of the tunes on which Louis plays invigorating and swinging solos.

Duke Ellington recorded with Louis and his All Stars in 1961 and produced a number of memorable performances on *Mood Indigo, Cottontail, Black and Tan Fantasy, Drop Me Off at Harlem* and many other tunes associated with Ellington. Allegro ALLR 800, 811 (in the US, Roulette RE-108).

Although Louis began increasingly to pace himself during the mid-1960s, a number of good albums were issued. Particularly notable is Mercury MCL 20083, 'Louis', with a front line including Tyree Glenn on trombone and Buster Bailey, Louis's old colleague from his days with Oliver and Henderson, on clarinet. Louis sings rather more than he plays on this agreeable album. When called upon he still hits those high notes and Glenn plays well, but Buster Bailey is under-utilized. However, *Tin Roof Blues, Tyree's Blues, Pretty Little Missy* and *Bye 'n' Bye* find the band and Louis riding along in fine form.

London SH-R 8190 (in the US, MCA 538), 'Hello Dolly', is another album of similar vintage featuring clarinetist Joe Darensbourg and Big Chief Russell Moore on trombone. Again Louis's trumpet playing is well paced and his singing is a joy. His zest for life is well expressed on this album and he still manages to amaze with his assured trumpet playing.

'What a Wonderful World', Stateside SL10247, made in 1966 and 1967, has only brief forays by Louis on trumpet but his singing takes on even greater expressiveness, perhaps due to the restricted nature of his playing. When he does play he keeps within the limitations of the middle register yet still manages to sound impressive.

Louis's final recordings find the great warrior now unable to play his beloved horn but still able to give supreme examples of jazz phrasing in his vocal performance. Philips 6369, 'Louis and His Friends' affords a last chance to appreciate Louis's overwhelming personality. *What a Wonderful World, My One and Only Love* and *Mood Indigo* are full of the Louis magic. His horn may have been silenced but his musicianship was still undiminished. This is jazz singing at its finest.

Louis Armstrong was a true genius of jazz, an inspiration to generations of musicians and jazz fans. His recordings are a lasting testimony to an inspired musician and a generous soul.

BIBLIOGRAPHY

Allan, Walter C. and Brian Rust — *King Joe Oliver* (London: Mayflower, 1975)

Armstrong, Louis — *Satchmo—My Life in New Orleans* (New York: Prentice-Hall, 1954; London: Peter Davies, 1955)

Barker, Danny with Alyn Shipton — *A Life in Jazz* (London: Macmillan, 1986)

Bechet, Sidney — *Treat it Gentle* (New York: Hill & Wang; London: Cassell, 1960)

Bigard, Barney with Anne Judd — 'Barney Goin' Easy', *Jazz Journal*, Vol.20, No.9, 1967.

Blassingame, John W. — *Black New Orleans* (Chicago: University of Chicago Press, 1973)

Boulton, David — *Jazz in Britain* (London: Allen, 1958 and New York: Scribner, 1958)

Braff, Ruby — 'In My Opinion', *Jazz Journal*, Vol.18, No.2, 1965.

Brecker, Randy — 'In My Opinion', *Jazz Journal*, Vol.22, No.3, 1969.

Buerkle, Jack V. and Danny Barker — *Bourbon Street Black* (New York: Oxford University Press, 1973)

Carey Mutt — 'New Orleans Trumpet Players', *Jazz Music*, Vol.3, 1946.

Cerulli, Dom, Burt Korall, and Mort Nasatir — *The Jazz Word* (London: Dobson, 1963)

Charters, Samuel B. — *Jazz: New Orleans 1885-1963*. (New York: Oak, 1963)

Charters, Samuel B. and Leonard Kunstadt — *Jazz. A History of the New York Scene* (New York: Schirmer, 1979)

Clayton, Buck with Nancy Miller Elliot — *Buck Clayton's Jazz World* (London: Macmillan, 1986)

Collier, James Lincoln — *Louis Armstrong* (London: Michael Joseph, 1964; New York: Macmillan, 1965)

Condon, Eddie and Thomas Sugrue — *We Called it Music* (New York: Holt, 1947); London: Davies, 1948)

Dance, Stanley — *The World of Earl Hines* (New York: Schribner, 1977)

Dance, Stanley	'Lightly and Politely', *Jazz Journal,* Vol.7, No.7, 1954.
Dance, Stanley	'Lightly and Politely', *Jazz Journal,* Vol.34, No.8, 1971.
De Radzitsky, Carlos	'Louis Armstrong at Brussels 1934', *Pickup,* Vol.2, 1947.
Driggs, Franklyn S.	'The Story of Harry Dial', *Jazz Journal,* Vol.11, No.12, 1958.
Driggs, Franklyn S. and Thornton Hagert	'Jerome Don Pasquall', *Jazz Journal,* Vol.17, No.4, 1961.
Foster, Pops	*Pops Foster* (Berkeley: University of California Press, 1971)
Gara, Larry	*The Baby Dodds Story* (Los Angeles: Contemporary, 1959)
Giddens, Gary, ed.	'Armstrong at 85' *Village Voice* (New York), 27 August 1985.
Gillett, Charles	*The Sound of the City* (New York: Outerbridge & Dienstfrey, 1970; London: Sphere, 1971)
Goddard, Chris	*Jazz Away From Home* (London: Paddington, 1979)
Goffin, Robert	*Jazz: From the Congo to the Metropolitan* (New York, Da Capo, 1975)
Goffin, Robert	*Horn of Plenty: The Story of Louis Armstrong* (New York: Da Capo, 1977)
Hadlock, Richard	*Jazz Masters of the 20s* (New York: Collier-Macmillan, 1965)
Hague, Douglas	'Louis Play the State House', *Jazz Journal,* Vol.11, No.4, 1958.
Halberstam, David	'A Day With Satchmo', *Jazz Journal,* Vol.10, No.8, 1957.
Haskins, Jim	*The Cotton Club* (New York: Random House, 1977; London: Robson, 1985)
Hodges, Johnny	'In My Opinion', *Jazz Journal,* Vol.17, No.8, 1964.
Houlden, David	'All Stars Past and Present', *Jazz Journal* Vol.11, No.3, 1958.
Israel, R.A.	'Louis Armstrong at Town Hall', *Pickup,* Vol.2, No.7, 1947.
Ives, David	'Claude Jones', *Jazz Journal,* Vol.15, No.6, 1962.

Jones, Max and John Chilton	*Louis: The Louis Armstrong Story* (Boston: Little, Brown, 1971; London: Mayflower, 1975)
Kaminsky, Max and V. E. Hughes	*My Life in Jazz* (New York: Harper and Row; London, Deutsch, 1963)
Kimball, Robert and William Bolcom	*Reminiscing with Sissle and Blake* (New York: Viking, 1973)
Lesberg, Jack	'Back O' Louis', *Jazz Journal,* Vol.23, No.7, 1970.
Levin, Floyd	'Ed "Montudie" Garland—Legend of Jazz', *Jazz Journal,* Vol.32, No.5, 1979.
Lion, Lorraine	'Mr Armstrong and Mr Robbins', *The Jazz Record,* No.39, 1945.
Lomax, Alan	*Mister Jelly Roll* (New York: Groves; London: Cassell, 1956)
Lyttelton, Humphrey	*I Play As I Please* (London: MacGibbon and Kee, 1957)
Lyttelton, Humphrey	*Second Chorus* (London: MacGibbon and Kee, 1958)
Manone, Wingy and Paul Vandervoort II	*Trumpet on the Wing.* (London: Doubleday, 1964)
McCarthy, Albert J.	*Louis Armstrong* (London: Cassell, 1960; New York: Barnes, 1961)
McCarthy, Albert J.	*The Dance Band Era* (London: Spring, 1974)
McCarthy, Albert J.	*Big Band Jazz* (New York: Putnam; London: Barrie and Jenkins, 1974)
Meryman, Richard	*Louis Armstrong: A Self Portrait* (New York: Eakins, 1971)
Mezzrow, Mezz and Bernard Wolfe	*Really The Blues* (New York: Random House; London: Secker and Warburg, 1946)
Morgenstern, Dan	'Pops in Perspective', *Jazz Journal,* Vol.15, No.5, 1962.
Norris, John	'One Sweet Letter From You', *Jazz Journal,* Vol.10, No.3, 1957.
Ostransky, Leroy	*Jazz City* (Englewood Cliffs, N.J: Prentice-Hall, 1978)
Owens, Frank	'Rudy Powell', *Jazz Journal,* Vol.23, No.6, 1970.
Panassié, Hugues	*Louis Armstrong* (New York: Da Capo, 1979)
Ramsey, Frederic, Jr, and Charles Edward	*Jazzmen* (New York: Harcourt Brace, 1939; London: Sidgwick

Smith	and Jackson, 1958)
Reeves, Edward M.	'Chicago in the Twenties', *Jazz Journal,* Vol.14, No.4, 1961.
Reeves, Edward M.	'Chicago in the Twenties', *Jazz Journal,* Vol.14, No.5, 1961.
Standish, Tony	'Joseph Robichaux—The Early Days', *Jazz Journal*, Vol.12, No.4, 1959.
Schuller, Gunther	*Early Jazz* (New York: Oxford University Press, 1986)
Scully, Arthur	'The Building Nobody Wanted', *Jazz Journal,* Vol.23, No.1, 1970.
Shapiro, Nat and Nat Hentoff, eds.	*Hear Me Talkin' To Ya* (New York: Rinehart; London: Peter Davies, 1955)
Simmen, Johnny	'Mr Trumpet Man—Frank Galbreath', *Jazz Journal,* Vol.23, No.11, 1970.
Simon, George T.	*The Big Bands* (New York: Macmillan, 1971; London: Collier Macmillan, 1974)
St Cyr, Johnny	'Jazz As I Remember it', *Jazz Journal,* Vol.19, No.9, 1966.
Vandervoort II, Paul	'The King of Riverboat Jazz', *Jazz Journal,* Vol.23, No.8, 1970.
Westerberg, Hans	*Boy From New Orleans* (Copenhagen: Jazz Media, 1981)

INDEX